Visions and Voices

Visions

and

Voices

JONATHAN COTT

A Dolphin Book
Doubleday
New York
1987

Library of Congress Cataloging-in-Publication Data
Cott, Jonathan.
     Visions and voices.
     Contents: Peter Brook—Oliver Sacks—Marie-Louise von Franz—[etc.]
     1. Interviews. 2. Intellectuals—Interviews.
I. Title.
CT120.C68   1987   920   87-6750
ISBN 0-385-24144-5

Contents

Preface

"I'd like to tell you the most important thing that ever happened to me," the Spanish poet Antonio Machado (1875–1939) once stated. "One day when I was still quite young, my mother and I were out walking. I had a piece of sugarcane in my hand, I remember—it was in Seville, in some vanished Christmas season. Just ahead of us were another mother and child—he had a stick of sugarcane too. I was sure mine was bigger—I knew it was! Even so, I asked my mother—because children always ask questions they already know the answer to: 'Mine's bigger, isn't it?' And she said, 'No, my boy, it's not. What have you done with your eyes?' I've been asking myself that question ever since."

It was Machado who also asserted that "Today, just as yesterday, the job of the eyes, the eyes in the head and in the mind, is to see." And nothing could be more truly said about the ten persons interviewed in this book, all of whom have endeavored to see things with their eyes wide open, and whose body of work is a reflection of their insight, intensity of attention, and clear-sightedness. Several of the interviews presented here were occasioned by a specific opening of a play or a movie (Peter Brook's *Carmen* and *Mahabharata*, Federico Fellini's *And the Ship Sails On)* or the publication of a book (Carolyn Forché's *The Country Between Us*, Oliver Sacks's *The Man Who Mistook His Wife for a Hat and Other Clinical Tales)*. But in these conversations, as well as in the other ones included here, I have always tried to deal with broader and more inclusive issues and subjects.

In my previous collection of conversations, *Forever Young*, I wrote: "Certainly in an interview, the act of glimpsing and sensing requires, on the part of both interviewer and interviewee, a delicate balance between 'seeing through' and 'seeing between,' a balance between openness and a respect for the mysteries and boundaries of personality.

"Needless to say, you cannot engage in this kind of interchange without admiring and delighting in the person to and with whom you are speaking. In an era when the sententious anecdotes and platitudes of late-night talk show celebrities—hardly disguising a pandemic sense of *tedium vitae*—dominate not only television but also the publishing media, it sometimes becomes hard to notice the multitude of men and women around us doing innovative and inspiring work—among them the persons in this book. All of them share a childlike aliveness to the feelings of the world and to the world of their feelings, all of them persevering, in spite of shifting fads and fashions, in the belief in and the exploration of that mysterious area where, in the words of the painter Joan Miró, 'creation takes place and from which there flows an inexplicable radiance that finally comes to be the whole human being.' "

Some things (and situations) don't change; and I have no reason to change the opinion I set forth in 1977 when *Forever Young* was published—exactly ten years ago. The anecdotes and platitudes endure. But so does the innovative and inspiring work of those who have retained their ability and courage to see.

As the poet Carolyn Forché remarks in the following pages about her two-year sojourn in El Salvador between 1978–80: "I was once driving past rows of cotton fields—all I could see on either side of the highway for miles was cotton fields, and it was dusty and hot, and I was rolling along thinking about something in my usual way. . . . But I didn't see *between* the rows, where there were women and children, emaciated, in a stupor, because pesticide planes had swept over and dropped chemicals all over them, and they were coughing and lethargic from those poisonous clouds. . . . There they were, and I hadn't seen them. I had only seen cotton and soil between cotton plants, and a hot sky—I saw the thing endlessly and aesthetically, I saw it in a certain spatial way. So I had to be *taught* to look and to remember and to think about what I was seeing."

In his book *Honey from the Rock: Ten Gates of Jewish Mysticism*, Rabbi Lawrence Kushner declares that "we are each different fragmentary manifestations of the Holy One Himself. And . . . the ultimate unification cannot occur until every single soul has become fully aware. . . . We are the result of the desire of awareness,/And the prayer of the

8

Creator,/To comprehend itself." And as he concludes the discussion with me that appears in this book: "Ultimately all we have is awareness. That's our only hope. Eyes wide open. Made for wonder."

Or as Sam Shepard expressed it when he signed my copy of his play *A Lie of the Mind*—and above his name wrote the words: *"Vamos a ver."*

"Let's go take a look."

JONATHAN COTT
New York City, 1987

Acknowledgments

Most of the conversations in this book have previously appeared, in shorter and slightly different form, in the following publications: *Ballet Review, Débat, L'Illustrazione Italiana,* Los Angeles *Times, New Age Journal, The New York Review of Books, Parabola, Rolling Stone.* And I am grateful to the following editors who originally edited some of these conversations: Jean Callahan, Christine Doudna, Susan Murcko, Robert Silvers, Philip Zaleski.

Special thanks to Bonnie Barrett (of CBS Records), Jane Emerson (of Ballet Society, Inc.), Nancy Hartman (of IRCAM), Mary Ellen Mark, Harry Mattison, Tom Miller, David Powers, Jeff Rosen, and George Wagner (of the Jung Institute, Los Angeles) for their help in obtaining the photos appearing here.

Most of all, I would like to thank Michael Carlisle, Jim Fitzgerald, Casey Fuetsch, and Jane and Jann Wenner for making this book possible; and, of course, the ten artists, doctors, and teachers who allowed me to interview them in the first place—and whose book this really is— for their inspiring visions and voices.

Peter Brook

THE LATE ENGLISH CRITIC KENNETH TYNAN WROTE THAT AT THE age of five, Peter Brook—indisputably one of the great theater directors of our time—inherited his brother's teddy bear, "an obese animal much prized for its ability to growl." "Within an afternoon," Tynan relates, "[Brook] had ripped it apart to find out where the noise came from: It never growled again, but at least he knew how it had growled." In the same year, Tynan adds, Brook was given "a fully equipped modern theater, and his childhood abruptly ended." But like a child, Peter Brook has never given up searching for or asking the most basic questions about his craft: "What is a play? What is character? Why act? Why go to the theater?"

After creating and taking on tour some of his greatest large-scale productions—*Titus Andronicus, King Lear, Marat/Sade, A Midsummer Night's Dream*—Brook, who had previously been based in London, moved to Paris. In 1970 he founded his International Center of Theater Research, where he worked, not with star actors like Laurence Olivier, John Gielgud, Paul Scofield, and Glenda Jackson (as he had done previously), but with an ensemble of unknown international performers who had the opportunity of taking advantage of Brook's lengthy rehearsal sessions and experimental techniques—reminiscent, in part, of the work of Antonin Artaud, Bertolt Brecht, and Jerzy Grotowski. Out of the workshops at this center came productions that featured a stage almost bare except for stones and gravel and whose actors used only a few props and occasional masks, resulting in some of Brook's most inspired work—*Ubu Roi, The Ik,* and, most astonishing of all, *The Conference of the Birds* (based on the twelfth-century Sufi story of a flock of birds undertaking a voyage in search of God)—proving that in the simplest of theatrical environments one could truly make the mysterious and the invisible incarnate.

In 1972 Brook took his troupe, in Land Rovers, on a 100-day, 8,500-mile journey through Africa where, in various villages and towns in

Algeria, Mali, Niger, Dahomey, and Nigeria, the actors would roll out a carpet in desert, forest, temples, or on dirt roads and then perform and improvise scenes from *The Conference of the Birds* for the local tribespeople. (Brook has suggested that all one needs to create theater is a person walking across an empty space with someone else watching, and that all that is required to create a ceremony, as in Haitian voodoo, is "a pole and people.")

Using his stripped-down aesthetic, Brook (in collaboration with music director Marius Constant and writer Jean-Claude Carrière) brought to New York City in 1983—after a successful two-year run in Paris—his eighty-minute version of *La Tragédie de Carmen. Carmen,* of course, tells the story of the amoral gypsy girl and her bewitched and ill-fated Spanish officer-lover, Don José. Made popular by Bizet's 1875 opera, which was in turn based on Prosper Mérimée's novella, the story rivals *Romeo and Juliet* as the most popular, oversung, and overtold work about obsessive love ever created. Yet even today it continues to inspire a musical like *Carmen Jones* and a film like Jean-Luc Godard's beautiful *Prénom Carmen.* Drawing on both Mérimée and Bizet, Peter Brook's version used only four singing roles, three speaking parts, and a chamber orchestra of fifteen musicians playing behind the singers. And, as usual, Brook, avoiding any intimation of the proscenium arch, had the events of the tragedy take place in sand and gravel and pebbles—allowing us to imagine, as no spectacular sets would, the idea and soul of Seville.

Theater critics generally loved this compendious "modern tragedy," while opera critics uniformly hated the "bastardized" production. But as Brook, speaking of orchestral musicians, once stated: "We recognize that a magical thing called music can come from men in white ties and tails, blowing, waving, thumping, and scraping away. Despite the absurd means that produce it, through the concrete in music we recognize the abstract, we understand that ordinary men and their clumsy instruments are transformed by an art of possession." And this, in fact, has been the aim of all of Peter Brook's extraordinary work.

Brook's work also includes a number of important movies. In addition to film versions of his productions of *Marat/Sade, King Lear,* and *Carmen,* he directed *Lord of the Flies* and *Meetings with Remarkable Men,* based on the book of G. I. Gurdjieff. It was, in fact, Gurdjieff who once said, "We think that if a man is called Ivan, he is always Ivan. Nothing of the kind. Now he is Ivan, in another minute he is Peter, and a minute later he is Nicholas. . . . You will be astonished when you realize what a multitude of these Ivans and Nicholases live in one man. If you learn to observe them, there is no need to go to a cinema." And ironically, both in his cinema and his theater, Peter Brook, through his characters and his powers of observation, has explored this truth and, at the same time, has tried to awaken his audiences from their habitual singleness of vision. Indeed, meeting this remarkable director, one is immediately struck by his alertness, attentiveness, curiosity, bedrock common sense, sense of self, and gentle but pointed sense of humor.

*   *   *

Bob Dylan once sang: "He not busy being born is busy dying." I mention that to you because you once wrote: "In the theater every form once born is mortal, every form must be reconceived." You have continually used words like "imitation," "preservation," "fixing," and "conditioning" to suggest the deadliness of much contemporary theater.

I remember when we were working years ago in California with the *campesinos.* We used a carpet—the carpet was the actual area where everything began and ended—and we were doing improvisations that lasted a minute or a minute and a half. One saw that the actor in that moment had the possibility of making something out of nothing, making it live. I remember one of the participants drawing everyone's attention to the fact that there was a birth and a death in it, and that the moment he finished, its life cycle was over.

At the same time, theater can't be *identical* to life. In the sixties, especially around 1968, there was a tremendous feeling that theater must *become* life, and so in the end there was no difference between performance and nonperformance or between a theater and a street event—which led to the point where you lived your own theater and where political events were taken to be theater.

But that just becomes verbiage and pure semantic play. Although theater *is* life, it is so in a specially concentrated form that reveals certain elements smudged up and covered over in everyday life. What is important is the capacity and necessity in the theater for something continually to be born again.

When I've written and talked about the "Deadly Theater," I've meant that for the audience and for the participants it is no longer serving the life-giving purpose for which, obviously, it came into existence. So that the Deadly Theater (it's a form of theater that is hanging on—God knows why—by inertia) is adding one more drop to the dying process rather than one more spark to the living one.

But one could take this one stage further, and say that, in fact, the two processes intermingle and coexist in a very complex and mysterious way. All the processes which seem to belong to the dying end of the spectrum can actually serve the life-giving one. Like repetition. Repetition can be the outward symptom of something that goes deeper and deeper into sclerosis. Or it can be the springboard on which the lively movement has to lean. One sees that the very capacity to recreate a performance—one sees this in music and in theater—only begins when a form is there in a sufficiently precise shape. It's like water flowing through a pipe: The fact that the pipe has to be more solid than the water brings us back to the central question of form. The whole of human existence depends on forms. They are our friend and our enemy, and without form there can be no life.

You once wrote: "Everything in opera must change, but in opera, change is blocked." In your new version of **Carmen,** *you have certainly made some changes in the Bizet opera. How do you now feel about opera as a "form"?*

The opera started five thousand years ago with people making noises as they came out of their caves. And out of those noises come Verdi and Puccini and Wagner. There was a noise for fear, for love, for happiness, and for anger—that was one-note, atonal opera; that's where it all began. At that point it was a natural human expression, and that turned into song. And, at some later time, that process became codified, constructed, and turned into an art. So far, so good. But at a certain moment, the art form became frozen; it began to be admired *because* it was frozen, and operagoers began to express a tremendous admiration for art as artificial.

The disease of the artificial gives very good results for the moment, and so you have beautiful and stylized works by Monteverdi and Gluck. Then you come to Mozart and find a perfect marriage between the artificial and something that's fully alive—here's an example of the rigid pipe and the water flowing through it. But gradually the attention begins to go more and more to the artificial until suddenly you're into sclerosis. Suddenly, that pipe is taking all the attention and less and less water is trickling through it, until you get a fundamentally unwell and crazy society in which people forget that pipes were put into buildings for the purpose of letting the water through and now consider them to be works of art. People knock the walls down and go into buildings to admire the piping and totally forget their original purpose and function.

18

This is what has happened in many art forms, and the opera is the clearest example.

Carmen is a gypsy, and in Mérimée's afterword to his novella, from which Bizet's opera is derived, he points out that Romany—the language of the gypsies—has had its roots traced back to India. The French writer René Guénon has written: "In Latin, verses were called Carmina, *a name connected with their use in the accomplishment of rites, for the word* carmen *is identical with the Sanskrit* karma, *which must be understood here in its special sense of 'ritual action.' " At the risk of imprisoning or "fixing" your interpretation of* Carmen, *it seems to me that the idea of "ritual action" seems to be at the heart of your production, and even of other people's recent versions of this work.*

I think you're absolutely right, and this is probably one of the reasons why *Carmen* has had this worldwide appeal. Unlike Verdi's *La Forza del Destino*, which talks about destiny in its title and has destiny music in it, the Carmen story essentially *is* a karma tale—I think that's absolutely true. Perhaps we could call the work *The Tragedy of Karma!*

The reason that Carmen and Don José are locked in their tragedy is that, fundamentally, each one is interested only in himself. Eventually, both of them transcend something, but not the bounds of egocentricity. Both of them ultimately take their love affair, their passions, their feelings as the whole universe. But there is something beyond even the greatest passion. And if either of them were aware of that, then *that* would liberate them. And that's where we come back to the question of karma. Mahatma Gandhi, for instance, may well have found himself, at one point in his life, in the situation of Don José. But his karma would not have been at the same level as Don José's, because at the moment when he could have killed his Carmen he would have recognized that there was something more in the world to serve than his own passions. And that's what would have liberated him.

It's strange that the character of Carmen is obsessed by both the idea of destiny and the idea of freedom.

I think that one of the very interesting aspects of *Carmen*, which every audience feels without analyzing it, is that Carmen in her behavior *isn't* free. The fact that she hates authority, kicks policemen in the balls, and does everything to despise ordinary structures isn't real freedom. That is simply her conditioning against another conditioning. She is a complete nonconformist and rebel in ordinary society, but within the gypsy society, she's completely conformist because that society has a different lifestyle. Everyone who, during the past twenty-five years, rebelled against the rigidly conformist Establishment, reacted out of one conditioning and plunged into another set of conditionings. In the sixties one saw this clearly. There were two mirror images, each one thinking itself superior and freer than the other and each equally conditioned.

That isn't where Carmen's freedom lies. Having seen the way her destiny is going, having seen that her nature and conditioning are going to make it impossible for her to compromise—because what is essential to her is a taste of freedom, the freedom to be true to herself, which means that she cannot betray herself—Carmen cannot take the easy and cheap way out. And yet she's intelligent and intuitive and perceptive enough to know that this is at the price of death. So her great and one and only act of freedom is to take responsibility for herself, totally, at an enormous price. And this is what makes a tragic hero.

Guénon also states that, by degeneration, the word carmen *eventually took on the meaning of "spell," and that magic is the last thing to be left behind when traditions disappear. It's interesting that in your production of* Carmen, *the heroine is deeply involved in magic. In fact, we first see Carmen—and it's a haunting first vision—covered in a cloak and hidden like one of the Fates, extending her hands from under her coverings and dealing out the cards of destiny.*

That's marvelous. If I'd known about Guénon, I could have said that I worked from that to illustrate these ideas. But do you know where I got that first image of Carmen from? While I was preparing this production, I went to Colombia and visited the Gold Museum of Bogotá where they have some mummies from Incan times. I suddenly saw something that took my breath away—it was a figure as you described it—a woman, a sort of skeleton from Incan times, with a withered hand and with that type of canvas and a rope wrapped round her. I looked at her and I knew that that was the essential Carmen. I took a photograph and brought it back to show my collaborators, who thought exactly the same thing. And that was our actual starting point.

Carmen *is a ritual that ends in death. And the fact that so many directors and filmmakers and opera producers are doing versions of* Carmen *right now might suggest that the rituals we tend to accept and even expect today seem to reflect a sense of disintegration rather than of renewal.*

But because of the element of positive acceptance, *Carmen* is not a morbid work. At a time when we're surrounded by death and slaughter and meaningless killing, there is something that entices us by a work that is *not* an expression of blind slaughter. Unlike, for instance, the rather dangerous Japanese cult of love and death as being something beautiful—death as a sort of splendid erotic experience, the ultimate orgasm. That, I think, is a very dangerous intellectual fantasy that Japan launched on the world after losing the war [laughing]. Because it's one thing to face death and another thing to woo death. Carmen isn't sick in that way, she hasn't got a death wish any more than does Don José. They're not Yukio Mishima characters. When, at the end, Don José has killed Carmen, the last thing you see is him looking straight ahead. And, to me, he is at that moment stoically facing a proper realization of who he is. I think that that is why an audience, at that point, feels there is something of stature in him. And that's why one doesn't feel the end as sordid because you discover a Don José who has, in a sense, got somewhere and become a *mensch*.

Your version of Carmen *takes place in sand and gravel and dust. And many of your productions have simply been performed on Persian and Indian carpets. You once even mentioned that theater can occur when just one person steps onto a carpet and someone else is there to witness that action.*

What creates the concentration of the theater is picking people out of life and putting them on a hot spot, somewhere where you can X-ray them. Which is why, on the whole—without generalizing—theater scenery does not help. I'm very fond of scenery, and I like designing it for the fun of it. But I don't think that in most cases it accomplishes what you're aiming for. It's not for nothing that the great periods like the Elizabethan have been those that did without scenery. In that way, you gain a greater X-ray concentration on something more interesting, which is the people.

On the other hand, in the cinema, both the person *and* his background are important at every moment. When you really want to isolate the person, then you go into a close-up. But in filmmaking, you can't remain long in close-up because you need to come back to the fact that the characters are, say, sitting in a restaurant—people in a specific environment and society. In theater, however, it's people alone.

Now, if you say that scenery is irrelevant, you'd be tempted to assert that the opposite is *nonscenery,* but this isn't true, either. Because if you actually take people and just put them on a board with a floodlight and a boxing ring, you then deny their humanity. You're picking them out of life and putting them on a laboratory table, but this is so dehumanized that the experiment is rendered invalid.

What you want is for them to be in the *texture* of life in the least localizing and the least constricting way. That's why I feel that in place of scenery, a support under and behind the person that has a texture is important.

The Bouffe du Nord, where we perform in Paris, is a ruined theater. All the walls are in tatters. But it has a tremendously warm, living atmosphere that a brand-new theater can't have. Ours is like the subway. I mean, it's got all of the graffiti of a hundred years on it, and you feel, as you do in the subway or in the lobby of the Chelsea Hotel, that an enormous amount of life has gone through it, which is the particular charm of ruins. And for the same reason we've used either a stone, earth, or a sand floor. Or, if it's an interior, something that is human and living and warm, like a carpet. I don't think these are aesthetic choices, but rather something that relates to finding the support, vertical and horizontal, that is in the same key as the substance of the human body. In Carmen we wanted *Spain* to be present in the way that corresponds to the story, which is desert, rock, sand . . . and not the colorfulness or picturesqueness of Spanish detail.

So the Bouffe du Nord, which has all the traces of things dying, is actually a setting that allows things to be born. And, likewise, the way you reduce and cut back the spectacular and picturesque—which is generally used to create the illusion of reality—allows you to get closer to a deeper reality.

I think that the other way, no one would believe it. Just a couple of months ago, I saw in India the most remarkable illustration of this. We were at an enormous theater-, ritual-, drama-performance about Kali [the Indian goddess of destruction], which lasted many hours and which involved an entire village. Kali appears—she's in a spectacular costume and makeup that's taken hours to put on—and she does a ferocious dance that, theoretically, is supposed to terrify everyone. Now, in the past, almost all of the people in the village experienced the true feeling of awe that Kali was actually amongst them. Today, of course, it's play-acting because everybody in the village, even the kids, has seen Indian movies and they know what it's all about. But everyone is still playing ball with the idea that it's scary.

At one moment, Kali, carrying a sword and surrounded by attendants throwing firecrackers, sets out of the village and starts walking up the main road. About a thousand of us followed her as she led this procession. We came to a crossroads, and as Kali stood there dominating everything, a Jeep came down the road. And I thought, What's going to happen? Who's going to give way? And, of course, without even thinking, Kali stepped back, as did her attendants, let the Jeep pass, and then walked forward again and carried on the ceremony [laughs].

Here you had the ultimate decadence of religious theater, because the genuine Kali would have thrown such a look at the Jeep that it would have stopped in its tracks and waited as long as the goddess wished. Or a smarter priesthood could have arranged to have had a James Bond Jeep there at which Kali would have just cast a glance and it would then have gone up in smoke just to impress the populace that she was still stronger than the modern age. But in front of a Jeep that wants to go along the highway, the little dancer playing Kali doesn't for a moment imagine that, even possessed by the goddess, she could hold up the traffic.

The gods just aren't what they used to be.

No, they respect traffic regulations.

I wanted to tell you a story that your story about Kali reminds me of. This one is about the founder of Hasidism, the Baal Shem Tov. It is said that when he saw misfortune threatening his people, he would go to a special place in the forest where he would meditate, light a fire, say a prayer, and the misfortune would be averted. Years later, one of his disciples went to that special place in the forest, but he didn't know how to light the fire; so he said the prayer, and, again, the danger was averted. Still later, another disciple, who knew neither how to light the fire nor how to say the prayer, saved his people because he at least could locate the secret place in the forest. But finally, years after that, another disciple spoke to God and said: "I am unable to light the fire, I do not know how to say the prayer, I can't even find the place in the forest. All I can do is tell the story, and this must be sufficient." And it was

23

sufficient because, it is told, God made human beings because He loves stories.

I'm really touched. That's a marvelous story. Going back to what I was saying earlier, I think if you try to start with a pretentious aim like re-creating a ritual, you can't do it. Because the place and the prayer and the way to light the fire are all forgotten. But you *can* start from the story.

At one point, I went through an experimental period and did things with the playwright Charles Marowitz like making a collage of *Hamlet* whose whole purpose was to take the story line out of that play. We did *Hamlet* the way Alexander Calder made mobiles, which was to take a bit here, a bit there, and put them in a kaleidoscope, so that people and images and strong moments and famous lines and actions *came* at you in a montage that had no story line. We tried to find other emotional lines, but we didn't have a narrative. I think that all those experiments eventually brought me to feel that the strongest concrete element that one can work from is telling stories . . . whether one is telling a story like *Carmen* or the *Mahabharata,* which I'm working on now. This Indian epic is so gigantic that it contains the whole cosmos in it. It's a great spiritual allegory. But both Jean-Claude Carrière, who's writing it, and I were convinced that if we started by trying to descend from the abstract —trying to descend from an overall cosmological view of it and bring that into the theater—we'd just make a lot of pretentious rubbish; that the way to best bring this epic to the West would be to go *outward,* by, first of all, telling its story. When Jean-Claude Carrière begins writing a scene, he has friends come over to his house and he starts telling them a story—without any commentary or explanation. And every time, the people are riveted and stay half the night.

But you can tell stories in a million ways. And I've observed that where you have great storytellers—as in the Middle East, for instance— they are very religious men. A great storyteller is never just a sort of out-of-work actor who has nothing else to do. He is somebody for whom storytelling is a vocation, a vocation that is related to his search through life. It is an act of devotion for him. Now, that doesn't make him tell a story in any pretentious or holy way. But it means that in the moment of *telling,* he is listening, with all that he has in him, to the *overtones* of the story, rather than stopping at the face value of the tale. And when a group of actors and I come together to work on something, I try to make us concentrate concretely and precisely on the story, and at the same time become, rehearsal after rehearsal, more open to its overtones.

For some people today, fairy tales have this same function.

That's very true. But there's one thing that theater teaches, which I think is very important, and that is—coming right back to our discussion about form—that at every moment of history and at every place geographically, there are forms that no longer speak and other forms that speak directly. For the majority, the word and image "fairy," which a hundred years ago set up a sort of opening, today sets up a resistance. When we did *A Midsummer Night's Dream*, for instance, what we had to discover was what form of imagery today would enable us to talk genuinely about fairies without setting up that antagonism we'd create if we brought on somebody in a fairy costume. That's why *E.T.*, for example —which is an old-fashioned fairy story—was a marvelous work. Without losing the innocence and the depth of a fairy story, Steven Spielberg rightly realized that if he'd made a film where there'd be leprechauns dressed with pointy hats and Pinocchio noses, he couldn't have commanded the same interest. And yet, essentially, he was telling a story about a leprechaun and about every child's wish to have one.

Your productions seek to find the mysterious in and through the visible. But it's been said that in ancient Egypt there were mystery plays dealing with divine deaths and resurrections; and that there were open and public parts of the performance that were held outdoors, while, at the same time, another secret play was being performed in the shrine of the temple. Do you believe in this distinction between, and the reality of, the "open" and the "secret" theatrical event?

I think that there are different—genuine, objective, absolutely clearly defined—levels of human beings and levels of understanding. But first let me say that I'm a great believer in theater being popular and accessible—one shouldn't think of "popular" as being a pejorative thing. But once you get a thousand people of all types in a theater—and if you do everything to make sure that it's as good a mix as possible—the range is infinitely richer and deeper than is popularly assumed. I always go back to the evidence of Shakespeare, who encompasses that very wide range between the popular at the lowest and the popular at the highest, knowing that his audience contains both the crudest and the most refined minds. And eventually the exceptionally perceptive mind can find a real, hidden, secret play in the hearts of *King Lear* and *Hamlet* and so on.

But beyond that, there is another level which is not popular, which is the next level of understanding and initiation. I wouldn't, for instance, expect to be invited to what would be a very private seminar at Princeton in which one Nobel prize laureate wants to speak to ten of his colleagues. And I wouldn't expect to be invited, partly because I would be bored out of my wits, and because I wouldn't have the least idea what any of his terms of reference are. And yet, the same Nobel prize winner could go on television and, if he has the gift for it, could present very difficult ideas in a way that could interest a million people.

So that's why I think that one must neither underestimate nor overestimate the theater. One mustn't reduce it to something that *can't* have a secret core, but a secret core that is in a way accessible to all who want to open themselves to it. So that, in this sense, the two images you mentioned—the "open" and the "secret"—coexist. One mustn't do what some theater people believe they can do, which is to turn the theater into a religious community. Because, in fact, the secret play is for those who are spiritually on a Princeton level; it is done by people of a very considerable level of understanding *for* people of that understanding. Anyone else who hasn't got it isn't necessarily excluded by locked doors but rather, as I said before, by the principle of boredom. I mean, I would open the doors wide for anyone who wants to enter the highest levels of secret experience, knowing that nobody's going to come. But we must still remember that an esoteric school is not a theater and a theater is not an esoteric school.

To go from the "secret" and "esoteric" to the extremely "open" and "available," I wanted to ask you about something fascinating, and almost prophetic, that you once wrote about in the late sixties. Suggesting that the "word" wasn't the same tool for dramatists that it once was, you asked: "Is it that we are living in an age of images? Is it even that we must go through a period of image saturation for the need for language to reemerge?" The proliferation of cable and videocassettes and music videos today seems to have pushed us even further in the direction of "image saturation" than it might have seemed possible in the sixties.

I think so. When I come to the United States, I always turn on the television set, but I never *watch* it; all I do is hop from channel to channel. When you're looking for something to stay tuned to, you see nothing but this familiar flow of imagery. Incidentally, I saw a film called *Liquid Sky* the other day, which I think is the worst thing I've ever seen. Unbelievable! Every image is drenched in *déjà vu*. It was made by some Russians who came to town and got culture shock. And what they're throwing back is all of the oldest psychedelic imagery you've ever seen—faces that suddenly turn into psychedelic colors and punk hairstyles. *Every* image in it is oversaturated.

Speaking of films, you once said that since movies flashed onto the screen images of the past (which, you added, is what one's mind does all through life), the cinema somehow seemed intimately real; but that since the theater asserted itself in the present, it was actually more real than our normal stream of consciousness, and possibly more surprising and disturbing. But you also once wrote that the cinema can give one a compressed sense of space and time, which allows for a more intensified way of seeing and therefore a possibility of transformed vision. Were you being a bit contradictory here?

I think I was talking in both cases of the possibilities and the difficulties of each form. I'll go one step beyond this. Cinema acts like the human consciousness in regurgitating old images, and that's one of the reasons why cinema-going is very lazy. Instead of closing one's eyes and seeing one's own recurrent images, something else is doing it for you and everything has been arranged very nicely. In that way, then, cinema-going is not provocative but is rather a great twentieth-century drug, making passive people even more passive. That's one side of it. And against that, the theater has the capacity of bringing the present right into being so it challenges something.

But the other side is also true. Because in the theater the characters are doing dangerous or difficult or amusing things, demanding nothing of you, and you sit there happily and watch it all going on. You're not involved. While the cinema has something happening that is *so* much in the present that you can't resist it. Because while the film images are fragments from the past, the actual physical movements seem to be happening here and now while you're looking at them. And that's why you could say that death and life—the frozen pipe and the running water—live in the cinema. There is a possibility of using, say, the unfolding music of the film to organize images in such a way that, as in poetry, the flowing sequence of those images becomes an action in the present; and thereby a person can be stimulated instead of being put to sleep.

Aside from combating this "sleep," you've insisted, in all your work, on concentrating on "the present in each moment."

That's the only place where anything can happen. It's the only place, ever. It can't happen yesterday or tomorrow. It can happen tomorrow, but only when tomorrow becomes the present.

[New York City, 1983]

II

For several years, Peter Brook has devoted himself to preparing a theatrical version of the ancient Indian epic, *Mahabharata*. The *Mahabharata* is one of the great all-encompassing works of world literature. Longer than the Bible, the *Iliad* and the *Odyssey*, and the plays of Shakespeare all put together, its (at one count) 274,778 lines of Sanskrit verse were gradually composed, accumulated, rearranged, and rescinded from about the fourth century B.C. to the third century A.D., interweaving theological, mythical, historical, political, ethical, medical, and folkloristic material. A compendium of Hindu legend and thought, it has been described as "a forest without end . . . a forest threaded by fables, confessions, stories, and secrets."

The focus of the *Mahabharata* is the dynastic quarrel between two groups of cousins—the Pandavas and the Kauravas—that culminates in global Armageddon. And inserted into this epic story is one of the most important and influential religious texts ever written, the *Bhagavad Gita (The Lord's Song)*, in which the Pandava warrior prince, Arjuna—standing in front of uncountable thousands of troops and horrified by the vision of the forthcoming slaughter—considers withdrawing from the battle, until his charioteer, the god Krishna, convinces him to fight.

Out of this density of material, the director Peter Brook, using a text adapted by Jean-Claude Carrière, has, like a master alchemist, transmuted the simplest theatrical elements of fire, earth, and water and fused the notions of action and dream to create a nine-hour dramatic event of grandeur, wisdom, beauty, and devotion. As performed by an international cast of twenty-one actors and five musicians from sixteen countries, the staged version of the *Mahabharata* enthralled sold-out audiences at the Bouffe du Nord theater in Paris for nearly eight months between 1985 and 1986. And an English-language version was presented in Zurich, New York City, and Los Angeles in 1987.

In his book *Classics Revisited*, the late poet and critic Kenneth Rexroth writes that "The reworking of [the *Mahabharata*] with every cultural change, and the Indian conservatism which cannot bear to throw anything out, result at last in the erosion of personality and human interest in the characters and their relations. The vast mass of contradictory moral ideas cancel each other out and leave only a lowest common denominator of motivation, an undramatic expediency and impassivity in the face of determinism. If all actions are separate but equal, there can be no drama."

When I visited Peter Brook in Paris in 1985, I asked him about Rexroth's comment—one that would seemingly make an undertaking like Brook's difficult if not foolhardy. The following was the director's response.

*   *   *

If you affirm with such totality, as Rexroth does, you're certain to miss something. India is so rich and so vast that you can do everything *except* affirm. What *is* true is that nobody can definitively say who wrote the *Mahabharata* or how it was written or what parts of it actually made up the original version. If you look at it simply in dramatic, poetic terms, you could say that it's a work of superhuman, more-than-Shakespearean genius, a work that builds to the most intense image—two vast armies standing still while the commander refuses to fight and his charioteer persuades him to do so. Perhaps the *Bhagavad Gita*, to which the story of the *Mahabharata* leads, comes from a later period. Perhaps many hands were involved in writing the whole text. But who cares? If you want to take the view that every single detail in it has some organic relation to everything else, you can do that. If you take the view that its story has accumulated through accretions, you can do that, too. Both are true. But what's clear is that there *is* a story. So what we did was not to change it but to extract *from* it in order to discover its real, living material. After all, if we'd dramatized the entire *Mahabharata*, the audience would be in the theater for more than a year! And in taking things away—but taking care not to stress one thing over another, simply eliminating what seemed to be irrelevant to the basic character and story line—what we then got was a work whose very nature was *totally* dramatic.

Because the basic story of the *Mahabharata*—and this was one of the main reasons I was drawn to it in the first place—is very different from almost any other epic in the sense that *everything* in it creates contradiction: All the characters and all of their actions are such as to smash any single moral idea. If you look at a particular character and say, "Ah, he's a good man!" something will immediately come along to disabuse you of that opinion. Somewhat troubled, you might then say, "Ah, yes, but *this* is a good idea!" and another event will suddenly counter that. Then you might notice a god and say, "Well, at least *that* god represents goodness!" and *that* evaluation will turn out to be suspect. Until you realize that the whole work expresses reality *through its own action.* How can you describe human interaction? The moment you try to do so, you're no longer describing it. How can you describe to somebody the turning of a wheel?

The essence of all religious thought is that it can't be captured in ordinary intellectual terms . . . it can only be experienced. This sense of unity is something too strong for human beings to live for more than a very short moment; so however intense it is, the notion of duality has to manifest itself, such that a person sees himself against the experience: There's the *experience,* the *me,* and then everything else follows. In this way, the need to interpret quickly arises; and with this need occurs the desire to affirm that something is right and something else is wrong. In no time, you're into the world of popes and clerics—it can't be avoided —and dogmatism takes over. And as people don't wish to be in the wrong, in the end they establish that they're right by means of torture, fire, murder.

Now, what happened with the *Mahabharata* was that at first the great Brahmans saw beyond the given forms of religious structures and sacrifices, but as time went by, as in all religions, the prophets were replaced by the clerics, and pure living thought hardened into dogma. So gradually the *Mahabharata* was rewritten in such a way that you now can come across an episode that explodes the idea of conventional right and wrong, followed by another passage—one that you can't help thinking was inserted a couple of hundred years later—that asserts there is really only *one* way of seeing and judging that earlier situation. And as you read on, you're faced with enormous lists that break behavior down into hard-and-fast categories—A, B, C, D, E, F, G. So the notion that nothing can be codified is now followed by the codifying of what can't be codified! And in our version of the *Mahabharata,* we've lifted out this code—we've taken the clerics out, so to speak—and returned to the basic material.

It's interesting, incidentally, that nothing criticizes this codifying mentality so powerfully than the *Bhagavad Gita* itself—the greatest of the great teaching works. If you look at the work closely, you realize that Krishna is warning the man who worships by form, not to think that it's enough to read the Vedas and to perform his sacrifices and so on

30

—an idea that is dynamite to the same orthodox mind, which, of course, holds the *Bhagavad Gita* in the highest esteem.

You see, unless one faces the question of what fate and destiny are, in Indian terms, one can't really enter into the human struggles between and among the contradictory urges and notions revealed in the *Mahabharata*—how can the desire, for example, of each person to fulfill his own desires, or the wish to find what is the "true" rather than the "untrue" action at any given moment be reconciled with the sense that everything is preordained.

Of course, this is only an apparent contradiction: How can an actor playing Hamlet make "To be or not to be" into a living and dynamic inquiry if the question's been decided before he starts the soliloquy?—although a good actor playing Hamlet both knows the outcome of the play and yet is able to enter into the urgency of this question at the moment when he experiences it in the action.

But let me give you an example from the *Mahabharata*. One of the most interesting and deeply sympathetic characters in it is Karna. He's someone born into two worlds: On the one hand, he's the son of a god —the son of Kunti and the Sun—born with a golden breastplate, and he has this glowing, beautiful nature; and on the other, this son of the Sun is brought up as the son of a coachman. So that he grows up with a profound inability to understand why, since he feels himself to be somebody extraordinary—and he feels this without vanity, since, like all human beings, he has an extraordinary potential—why is it that all the world slights him . . . why isn't he naturally recognized as extraordinary by his environment? And this lack of balance—plus the fact that he's deprived of a mother, which in modern terms could easily turn into bitterness, resentment, and anger—doesn't lead Karna to become, say, a terrorist; in fact, he's known for his generosity of spirit. But what he feels is total incomprehension . . . and the one focus for all his destructive energy is Arjuna, who is his brother, although he doesn't know it. In some sense, Karna is Arjuna's mirror image—Karna the person off-center, Arjuna on-center. But eventually one sees that this "focus" is part of an enormous pattern, for Karna's role is to bring Arjuna to his highest point, since if Arjuna didn't have an opponent of Karna's quality, he would never achieve what he does.

Krishna is a god, he is Vishnu, who comes to earth as a man—and he lives fully like a man, he makes love, he makes war, he's a politician, he's a charmer . . . but he is never distracted from his one aim, and that is to restore the balance of the universe. And here again what is paradoxical is that Krishna knows what is going to happen, because as a god there is nothing that can surprise him, nothing is unforeseen; and yet the entire action of his role as Krishna is that of reflecting, searching, maneuvering, using every intuition, every strategem, every ruse to outwit the enemy, the Kauravas, whom he knows must anyway lose. On a very simple level, one can say, as children do, "Well, if God knows what's going to happen, why doesn't He do this or that?" And here one finds the great divine paradox: Krishna *knows* but acts as though he *doesn't* know. As a god, he knows there's going to be a war, that it has to take place; and yet as a human being, he tries with total commitment to do whatever he can to prevent it—and in a key scene he meets Karna and tries to persuade him not to go to war by revealing to him that his enemy, Arjuna, is his brother. Krishna acts to prevent the inevitable in a deeply moving, human way and his action, objectively, is the reverse: to push the inevitable even more inexorably to its inevitable conclusion.

So here you have an incredibly complex set of tensions and contradictions that operate *through* the characters. For Krishna has to work by feeling out all of Karna's weak spots and then playing on them. Karna's great attribute, his strength—or is it his weakness?—is his ferocious loyalty. Were he to join his brothers, he would be disloyal to his friends. What is extraordinary is that in sticking to his roots, to his generosity, to his honesty, he is, conversely, also revealing the relativity of all human values, because for those sympathetic reasons he is condemning several million people to death.

So you see how these things turn themselves inside out: at the moment you think how magnificent it is that Karna is being true to himself, you have to face the truth that he is condemning the world to die. But Karna himself recognizes this, and says to Krishna: "I've seen it in my dreams—you're going to win this war, I know that I'm on the losing side." Yet if he's so self-aware, why can't he go beyond this? Why can't Krishna impel him to say: "To hell with all of this, only one thing matters to humanity—that there be no more war!"

And here you meet the essential question of destiny: Each person, superficially, is a million persons; but if you dig through sand and earth, you eventually reach bedrock, where you contact a person's central identity . . . you come upon the one thing that can't be changed. For at the very root, each human being *is* a type. Now this is easily misunderstood, and the word evokes "type" in a superficial sense—every Italian likes spaghetti, Mexicans have big mustaches. One must go through all the horrors of racist thinking and eventually discover that you've in fact come *back* to type: The absolute, essential Jew is *not* the same as the absolute, essential Chinaman; the essential man is *not* the same as the essential woman. We can, of course, point to the dreadful exploitations of these differences; but there *is* a pure male, which is one sort of planet, and a pure female, which is another planet—one neither better nor worse than the other—but they are not the same.

And it's only when the type is pure that the destiny becomes pure. To me it's very clear that although everyone has a potential destiny, not everybody lives it. And probably the idea of reincarnation is connected to this—you can live your life again and again and never meet your destiny . . . such that in one life you might be run over by a bus, in the second you might live to be eighty years old, and in the third you might be on the point of dying and are saved by a newly discovered antibiotic; yet in none of these lives have you been living your destiny. And the paradox is that our fate is *not* inevitable . . . our fate is our *truth*. And the closer we get to our truth, the more we see fate, not as this ridiculous notion of someone's writing something in a book and us simply walking like a zombie through the part, but as something magnificent . . . which is that of really becoming oneself.

Now to become oneself is the hardest task of all, requiring everything in life, including every battle. For me—and this is a personal reading—I see no contradiction between Krishna's knowing what is going to happen and his struggling to help each person go deeper, thereby making that person face choice after choice, until he reaches the point where there are no more choices left, and he is what he is. So if you look at that meeting between Krishna and Karna from this perspective, you can see that Krishna is honorably offering every single choice to Karna; and the more truly Karna responds openly to Krishna's provocation, the more he goes, step-by-step, deeper and deeper until he reaches the point where there is no more choice. And Krishna then has to say to him: "I can't touch you, you prefer the destruction of the earth, and so the earth is lost." And here Krishna expresses the ultimate tragedy of this god who recognizes the nature of human life and also the reality that even for him as a god there is no choice either.

The pinnacle of the *Mahabharata* is the *Bhagavad Gita;* but in our production, we don't present it or have it spoken—we just have Krishna whisper it to Arjuna. You don't get cured in a theater! But if you want to go further, there *is* the *Gita* . . . and the whole of the rest of your life to continue your search. As an Indian once said to me very simply: "The whole of the *Mahabharata* shows that one can't escape from the law of karma"—from one's patterns, in other words. "But the whole of the *Bhagavad Gita* is to say, yes, you can." Since reality and truth can't be defined, you can only trap them with snares. Seeing that they're fugitive and cunning, man long ago became more cunning still and invented contradiction as a tool to help reality appear.

I first encountered the *Bhagavad Gita* when I was working on the revue *US* in 1966. And we thought of an opening for that show, which we later decided not to use, that presented General Westmoreland, whom I thought at the time was *the* supreme villain for the simple reason that he gave himself the comfort of a moral position regarding the Vietnam War—he being the man who said, "I want my soldiers every day to be 100 percent human." Can you imagine? And we thought of showing him going into action, then suddenly stopping and saying what, if he really *were* 100 percent human, he *would* have said . . . namely: "Why should we fight?" If he had done that, how human we *would* have found him. How marvelous! Just imagine, in the middle of the Tet Offensive, seeing all the helicopters motionless in the sky, and the general saying, "Why should we fight and massacre our brothers?" And yet, of course, the whole of the *Bhagavad Gita* goes beyond what would seem for a human being to be that ultimate position.

When Prime Minister Margaret Thatcher was starting the Falklands War, I was in India; and an Indian said to me, "Ah, you see, Mrs. Thatcher has drawn the lesson of the *Bhagavad Gita*. She sees that you shouldn't hesitate, you must fight!" And I was appalled, because that comment revealed an important misunderstanding . . . and you can imagine how politicians and presidents could use Krishna as justification for their positions on nuclear war! But in fact the *Bhagavad Gita*'s idea is not that at all. In the action of the story, you see Krishna doing every simple human thing he possibly can to prevent the conflict; the Supreme Commander, Arjuna, also tries to avoid the war; and when this particular war becomes inevitable, then all the Pandavas accept to fight, not to assert their egos, but to play their role in a pattern that only Krishna can understand. Now, it's quite clear that when Mrs. Thatcher went to war, she was acting as Mrs. Thatcher, not Mrs. Thatcher *listening* with every molecule and every cell to something way beyond any of her own personal feelings or interests in the matter. And that's why the *Gita* must be rigorously understood, and not taken naïvely as a justification for war.

One realizes that Hinduism led Indian thought to the understanding that nothing—no human psychological event—can be separated from the vast texture of which it is a part; and that within the concept of action that everyone is continually involved in, there is always the latent question: "Is this the right action?" Which leads one to the notion of personal *Dharma* . . . so that one must ask: "Am I, at any given moment, going toward what is true in relation to my own essential meaning and reality? And how does being true or false to myself relate to every other human being's need to function in relation to the great *Dharma* of the entire universe?" And once you have this context, then one can see that the whole story of the *Mahabharata*—in which every character is being pulled by these two questions, with all the conflicts, confrontations, and contradictions that they entail—is, of course, endlessly dramatic.

[Paris, 1985]

Dr. Oliver Sacks

In 1926 an outgoing, carefree, and high-spirited twenty-one-year-old young woman, whom the British neurologist Dr. Oliver Sacks calls Rose R., began to have a recurring dream. And in this dream, in the words of Dr. Sacks, "she was imprisoned in an inaccessible castle, but the castle had the form and shape of herself; she dreamed of enchantments, bewitchments, entrancements; she dreamed that she had become a living sentient statue of stone; she dreamed that the world had come to a stop; she dreamed that she had fallen into a sleep so deep that nothing could wake her; she dreamed of a death which was different from death." Then one morning, after a night of dreaming this dream, Rose R. had difficulty waking up. Her family, who had come to her bedside, found their daughter lying in bed, unable to speak, her eyes turned to the wardrobe mirror. "And there," as Dr. Sacks tells us, "she saw that her dreams had come true."

Forty years later, in 1966, the neurologist discovered her, along with a group of other mostly stuporous and transfixed patients ("human statues, as motionless as stones") in a ward of a New York hospital where he had begun to work—the forgotten survivors of a rare sleeping sickness called *encephalitis lethargica* that had broken out during World War I in all parts of the world and that, having affected some five million people within twelve years, vanished as mysteriously as it had arrived.

In 1969 Dr. Sacks, after much deliberation, decided to administer to these patients a drug—used to treat Parkinsonism—called L-dopa. And suddenly, as if in a "miracle" story or fairy tale when the spell or enchantment has been broken, "there burst forth the wonder, the laughter, the resurrection of Awakenings. Patients motionless and frozen, in some cases for almost five decades, were suddenly able, once again, to walk and talk, to feel and think, with perfect freedom. . . . One could not witness such 'awakenings' without feeling their legendary and fantastic quality, without thinking of the Sleeping Beauty, Rip Van Winkle, and other fictional and mythological parallels. The first

39

awakenings nearly always gave intense and unmixed joy to the patients." (Oliver Sacks's accounts of these "rebirths" make up his book *Awakenings*—first published in 1973 and revised, expanded, and republished in 1983—one of the most profound, unsettling, compassionate, and beautifully written works of our time.)

But it soon became clear to Dr. Sacks that the side effects of L-dopa were bizarre and unpredictable, with each patient reacting to the drug in distinct and unique ways. Rose R., for example, now sixty four years old and unable to comprehend and accept the loss of forty-three years, "reblocked" herself and fell, so to speak, back into her sleep and trance.

Another patient, whom Oliver Sacks calls Margaret A.—she was born in 1908 and had suffered from the sleeping sickness since her early twenties—found herself, under the influence of L-dopa, propelled from one exteme behavioral state to another (depression-mania, coma-frenzy). As Dr. Sacks reported her plight at that time: *"Both* poles, indeed, may simultaneously occur, and Miss A. will declare—within two or three minutes—that she feels wonderful, terrible, can see perfectly, is blind, cannot move, cannot stop moving, etc. Her will is continually vacillating or paralyzed; she wants what she fears, and fears what she wants; she loves what she hates, and hates what she loves. . . . In the presence of excitement and perpetual contradiction, Miss A. has split into a dozen Miss A.s—the drinker, the ticcer, the stamper, the yeller, the swinger, the gazer, the sleeper, the wisher, the fearer, the lover, the hater, etc.—all struggling with each other to 'possess' her behavior. . . . The *original* Miss A.—so engaging and bright—has been *dispossessed* by a host of crude, degenerate subselves—a schizophreniform fission of her once-unified self."

A professor of clinical neurology at the Albert Einstein College of Medicine in New York and a consultant neurologist to a number of small New York hospitals, Dr. Oliver Sacks was born in London in 1933 into a medical family. (His mother was a surgeon and a professor of anatomy, and his father, now ninty-one [1985], still sees patients as a general practitioner.) A bearded, bespectacled, almost rabbinical-looking man, Dr. Sacks speaks with a gentle stammer and a veritable twinkle in his eye. ("When I ask some of my patients, 'How old are you?'—he comments with a smile—"they'll reply, 'You tell *me!'* ") Unpretentious, courteous, jolly, and humane, he is a doctor who embodies and combines the "old-fashioned" qualities of wisdom teacher, healer, and artist; who speaks openly and unembarrassedly about a "neurology of the soul"; and whose prose style displays a remarkable sense of grace, strength, exactitude, and passion.

Drawing on a deeply felt knowledge of neurology, physics, cosmology, philosophy, Jewish mysticism, literature, and music (his two favorite bedside books are the dictionary and the Bible, and he is fond of quoting the German poet Novalis's dictum: "Every disease is a musical problem, every cure a musical solution"), Oliver Sacks has published three books during the past several years: *Migraine*—an expanded and updated version of his pioneering 1970 study (and one which led Israel Rosenfield to call Sacks "one of the great clinical writers of the twentieth century"); *A Leg to Stand On*—an account of how, having torn the quadriceps tendon of his thigh, he embarked on a pilgrimage through the "broken mosaic world" of the *patient,* with all its ontological terrors and convalescent grace ("To become a true doctor," he quotes the French philosopher Montaigne, "the candidate must have passed through all the illnesses that he wants to cure and all the accidents and circumstances that he is to diagnose. Truly I should trust such a man"); and, most recently, *The Man Who Mistook His Wife for a Hat and Other Clinical Tales*—a best-selling collection of twenty-four almost Gogolian- and Borgesian-like case studies about seemingly "untreatable" brain-damaged persons—e.g., a man finds freedom from his uncontrollable tics, jerks, and grimaces only when he plays the drums or Ping-Pong ("Witty Ticcy Ray"); a woman who, though possessing the sensory faculties of her hands, can neither recognize nor identify any object that she touches ("Hands"); a man who, while able to see colors, shapes, and shades of brightness, has lost all conception of imagery or faces ("The Man Who Mistook His Wife for a Hat"); and an ex-sailor who, thirty years after being discharged from the Navy, finds it impossible to fathom the reality of persons or events appearing and occurring after 1945, and who is, for example, even unable to recognize Dr. Sacks himself from one moment's meeting to the next ("The Lost Mariner").

The philosopher and political scientist Hannah Arendt once wrote: "In acting and speaking, men show who they are, reveal actively their unique personal identities, and thus make their appearance in the human world." Yet in all these action-impaired patients, Oliver Sacks—through sympathy, dedication, patience, understanding, intuition, and faith—reveals how he has been able to discover and evoke "a living personal center, an 'I,' amid the debris of neurological devastation." And he has done so in a series of haunting tales that mix narration and meditation—as if to confirm Isak Dinesen's notion that "All sorrows can be borne if you put them into a story."

*   *   *

We sometimes read about certain patients who get so identified with their illnesses that they seem to be nothing but functions of them—like the Tourette's syndrome patient you refer to as "Witty Ticcy Ray," who says, "I consist of tics—there is nothing else."

Yes, that particular man suffered from all kinds of tics and grunts and involuntary cursing and shouting and stamping—it would attract outraged attention in the streets. And he came to me looking for a quick chemical answer, which I gave him: a drug called haloperidol (it's like L-dopa in reverse).

Now, he was obviously sensitive to the drug, but he had bad effects from it as well. And he came back to see me, very upset by the whole business, because the magic hadn't worked; indeed, the drug misfired, and many of his symptoms were worse. He then told me that he wasn't sure he *wanted* to be treated, saying, "I've had Tourette's since I was three. I consist of tics, and if you take them away I feel I won't be there." And it was at this point that he started referring to himself in the third person—not as "I" but as "Witty Ticcy Ray" or as the "Ticcer of Presidential Thruway." It was necessary for him to believe that there might exist a "nonticcy" identity. So a sort of imaginative and "existential" exercise was needed for some months until he felt he could face, enjoy, and even celebrate a life without tics. At that point we tried the same drug again, and it worked superbly . . . it's worked superbly ever since.

It is in this sense of treatment that one wonders why you didn't originally want to become a psychiatrist instead of a neurologist.

Of course I'm interested in the psyche and in being. But, finally, I'm much too interested in the organic—in the relation between body and mind, between organs and being. It is insufficient to consider disease in purely mechanical or chemical terms; it must be considered equally in biological or metaphysical terms. In my first book, *Migraine,* I suggested the necessity of such a double approach, and I continue to develop this theme in my present work. Such a notion is far from new—it was understood very clearly in classical medicine. In present-day medicine, by contrast, there is an almost exclusively technical or mechanical emphasis, which has led to immense advances, but also to intellectual regression and a lack of proper attention to the full needs and feelings of patients. I hope that I may go a bit further than my colleagues in trying to look at the relationship of the disorder to the individual, at the struggle to endure and to maintain identity. The construct is finally dramatic and existential—the individual struggles to carry on in the face of a changing physiology.

I'm fond of browsing in the etymological dictionaries, and it pleases me that "will" and "well" are a sort of etymological double. And I think that *being* well—and certainly *getting* well—may require a will. In the case of Witty Ticcy Ray, at first he didn't *will* wellness . . . maybe he willed illness, and the *will* had to change before the drug could work. I think that the will to live or not live—sometimes thought of as something metaphysical—is terribly real; and I see it all the time.

In certain sixteenth- and seventeenth-century English poems, there was a tradition of organizing verses of three stanzas in such a way that the first dealt with memory, the second with understanding, and the third with will. But if memory goes—as it does in many of your patients— what happens to understanding and will?

It seems to me that will is the deepest thing in our being. And even in profound dementias, when the slate seems to have been wiped clean, there's this urge—something I practically equate with life itself—that is suggested in the last words of Samuel Beckett's novel *The Unnamable:* ". . . you must go on, I can't go on, I'll go on."

But will also depends on identity and memory; and if these are undermined by disease, one may see a strange sort of will-lessness or indifference. . . . Some of this is touched on in "The Lost Mariner"— a story of a man with profound amnesia due to Korsakoff's syndrome. This man, who seemed to have lost his past and his future and all sense of personal continuity, also seemed to have lost his will as well. . . . And I also tell of a man ("A Matter of Identity") who had so lost his memory that he misidentified me as twenty different persons in the span of five minutes! And he would continually confabulate, invent stories— often very funny and brilliant stories—because, in some sense, he had lost his *own* story. One *must* have a story, one *must* have a narrative of one's life . . . otherwise one isn't alive.

I recently read a beautiful late essay by Freud called "Constructions in Analysis." And to Freud, a construction is not simply an interpretation, but rather a reconstruction of an early or repressed part of an infantile story—of how something was or might have been.

I think that medicine can't do without stories. This was the view of Hippocrates (who was supposedly the teacher of Thucydides); he said, in effect, that medicine couldn't be just science, it had to be history as well. And it's this insertion of history into science—this *conjunction* of personal narrative with physiology—that seems to me as essential in clinical medicine and clinical tales. The great Russian neuropsychologist A. R. Luria was a master in combining storytelling with science, and used to speak of "romantic science" in this connection.

There's a title of a play by Samuel Beckett—it's called *Not I*—that has always haunted me. And I'm especially interested in neurologic and organic problems that seem to destabilize the sense of "I" in some sort of way. In the case of the man I mentioned before who misidentified me as at least twenty different people, he was forced to invent scenes. Now, he was a part of every scene—one might say the only *stable* part of every scene. He began by seeing me as a customer. (In real life, he had worked in a delicatessen.) But then that broke down . . . it became clear that I wasn't a customer . . . and then he had to see me as someone else. But all of this kept breaking down. So, in *this* case, the attempted cure—the attempt to stabilize him—had in fact destabilized him, because all his stories were fictions. He needed his "true" story—but this he had lost. Whereas what Witty Ticcy Ray and I did together was to imagine and construct a possible life story—one not dominated by tics. And to that end, I acted as a kind of mirror that revealed his possibilities.

So your patients play an active part in their own treatment.

Yes, indeed. Some years ago I worked with a patient whose physical sense of balance had been so disturbed by Parkinson's disease that he walked with a precarious tilt to one side like a human Leaning Tower of Pisa. The man had been a carpenter, and when I showed him a videotape of his tilting walk, he was reminded of the spirit levels he had used in his work to tell whether a surface was straight. "Is there some sort of spirit level in the brain?" he conjectured. Parts of the inner ear are indeed like levels, and the man's homely analogy prompted a solution. We devised a pair of eyeglasses equipped with miniature horizontal levels extending forward from the bridge over the nose, and after some experimentation the man was able to use these spectacles to right his stance.

As a physician, how do you define your role in the patient's narrative?

Most of my patients are in homes for the aged and the chronically ill and suffer from the most severe forms of neurological damage. My work, my life, is all with the sick—but the sick and their sicknesses drive me to thoughts that, perhaps, I might not otherwise have. As Nietzsche said, "As for sickness, are we not almost tempted to ask whether we could get along without it?"

There's a part of me that almost *has* to organize clinical perception into a narrative, as well as theoretically. I tend to see most of my patients in the morning. Then, typically, I go for a walk in the New York Botanical Gardens. And while I'm there, I'm not consciously thinking about the patients I've just seen; but by the time I've returned to my office, the mass of things that have been told to me have taken the form of a story—a story that is the presentation of a problem, that investigates that problem, and that embeds all of my thoughts about it. Subsequently, I think, the patient comes to share the story, and the story gets modified. This comes back to what I was saying before about the need for a narrative. I think this need is absolutely primal. Children understand stories long before they understand trigonometry. And, for me, there is equally the need to tell a story and the need not to distort.

A friend of mine, who is a professor of pediatrics, says that, in her opinion, patients don't lie. And if they do, the lying is superficial and the truth is there on a deeper level. I do regard myself somewhat, sometimes, as a voice for the voiceless. And I feel that if my patients could speak, their individual stories would be what they would tell. Some of my students, incidentally, used to get a bit confused and would say to me, "Dr. Sacks, you talk like the patients and the patients talk like *you*" [laughing]. Now, it's true that I don't talk entirely like a neurologist and that I do talk partly like a storyteller. But, on the other hand, I don't think that that makes me less of a neurologist.

Hippocrates was called the father of medicine; but he was also the father of medical *stories*, the father of case history. He gave us words like "prognosis" and "prodrome"—words that indicate that illness *has* a story and a narrative. And I think that, as at old-fashioned medical schools, you should be able to open any patient's chart and find his or her story. Of course, there's always a complex mixture between the patient's story and the doctor's rendering of the story. And the more that one can put the patient's own words in quotes, the better. But then it all has to be deepened and suffused with, though, one hopes, not distorted or reduced by, a physician's interpretation. But this kind of storytelling has rather disappeared in the past forty years. What we now get are a series of anonymous cases, presented in terms of percentages and so on (which, of course, are important), but the *individual* doesn't come through.

The limits of set, mechanical testing were strikingly brought out with some patients I once worked with—identical twins of subnormal intelligence, but with extraordinary powers of calculating or "seeing" numbers, instantly able to state dates or days of the week anytime in the last or next forty thousand years ("The Twins"). These rather mechanical feats—which are startling, but not of *really* deep interest—had been well documented in articles and even exhibited on television. But there was something else far more mysterious, which I came across only by accident, by being with them, knowing them, quietly, for a long time. I was working then on a ward where they were confined. One day I came across them talking to each other, with strange secret smiles on their faces—and their conversation consisted of swapping and savoring six-figure prime numbers. When I realized this, I was able to join in—with the help of a book of prime numbers—and then they went up bit by bit to swapping twenty-figure primes. This was amazing, quite beyond my understanding, indeed inexplicable by any account of mind—and it was something I was, so to speak, *allowed* to see or allowed the twins to reveal by abdicating a purely mechanical or professional role and permitting them to feel at ease, spontaneous, and intimate, in a very personal communion and contemplation. I always try to see my patients as *individuals,* which is not always practiced in a strictly medical or psychological setting.

William Osler, who was a very great physician, once said that "To talk of diseases is a sort of *Arabian Nights* entertainment." And this might sound either frivolous or monstrous if one didn't know that it came from Osler. And one might wonder in what sense it is true and what Osler meant by this. In my understanding, I think that it has to do with the fact that not only has every person with an illness or injury a story, and that not only are these stories interesting and varied, but that they also often have a quality of myth, of fairy tale, of dream. What interests me is the intersection between fact and fable. And in what appear to be the bleak rooms of clinics and chronic hospitals, I hear sagas, I see victims, I observe heroes, I witness great strivings of the human spirit.

How did you happen to get so interested in the idea of story and narrative?

I don't exactly know, but I think it can in part be attributed to my mother. She was trained in neurology and anatomy; and, later, she became a professor of anatomy and surgery—she was, incidentally, the first Jewish woman to become a Fellow at the Royal College of Surgeons. Now, on the one hand, she loved anatomy, she loved minute detail . . . she had a tremendous feeling for this. I remember once saying that I had difficulty remembering the bones of the foot. And she said, "It's not a question of remembering but of understanding." And she drew me a foot—she drew me a whole *lot* of feet—and said, "Don't you see how the stresses must go and how it's like a bridge?" She immediately looked at it as an architect or like an engineer. But I couldn't see it; I didn't have that power.

So, she was my first tutor in anatomy, but she herself also loved to tell stories—rather disquieting ones, in fact, like D. H. Lawrence's "The Man Who Loved Islands" and Conrad Aiken's "Silent Snow, Secret Snow."

I've always associated your work with this latter story—about the little boy who, in the process of becoming autistic, sees and feels snow falling all around him when in fact it's sunny and springtime outside.

It's an extraordinary story, and what's so powerful about it, I suppose, is that on the one hand something terrible is happening to the boy, but it presents itself to him as a sort of sweetness.

I've been working mostly with older patients, yet, strangely, I just recently wrote up a story about a young man in his twenties ("The Autist Artist"). He had been variously described as idiotic and autistic, he had very severe epilepsy and temporal lobe seizures and brain damage, and there didn't seem to be any interaction with anything, until I took a copy of the magazine *Arizona Highways*, which I subscribe to because I love the desert. And, putting a pen in his hands, I opened up the magazine, showed him a photograph, and said, "Draw that!" And he immediately became sort of intense and quiet—the attendants had told me he wouldn't understand—and that was the beginning. His drawing revealed an extraordinary mixture of detail and comic exaggeration. In fact, in all of my work with autistic patients, the meeting point has never been in words, it's always been in play of one sort or another: one "meeting" was at the piano, another at a pool table. For I think that in the mode of play, one is no longer a composite of "drives," one is no longer driven at all.

I think that health resides in play or action; and whatever the problem, I try to bring out something central, something active, in all my patients. My story "Hands" is about this and nothing else—how, through being active, using them, a patient discovers she *has* hands.

This woman, who had long regarded her hands as useless lumps of putty, reached out one morning for a bagel. Impatient, hungry, instead of waiting passively and patiently, she acted—her first manual act in sixty years. After this act, progress was extremely rapid. She continued reaching out to explore the world. She asked for clay and started to make models; and eventually her attention, her appreciation, moved from objects to people.

I think of disease as "Humean" and health as "Kantian." The philosopher David Hume affirmed that we are "nothing but a bundle or collection of different perceptions, succeeding one another with inconceivable rapidity, and in a perpetual flux and movement." And in this way, Hume is driven to consider man as passive and a spectator and not as an experiencer or active agent. The notion of action is so ostentatiously and absurdly absent that it was necessary for someone like Kant to make the idea of action central.

Writing about the Japanese puppet play known as Bunraku, *Susan Sontag once commented that this kind of play shows us that "to act is to be moved." And I was thinking of Ida T. in* Awakenings *who, after taking L-dopa, says, "Wonderful, wonderful, I'm moving inside!"*

Even walking—something that would appear to be so mechanical, automatic, inexpressive, impersonal—is a movement of the soul. What is very characteristic of Parkinsonism, for example, is that the music of a style of walking goes away, and a peculiar, robotic, puppetlike quality takes over such that a person actually feels that he or she is "walked"— the person isn't the "walker."

I took Susan Sontag's remark to include the idea of being "moved emotionally."

Absolutely. I'm reminded of one of my patients who would be "moved"—literally—by music that touched some emotional spring. The emotional spring is also a motor spring.

When I was first studying biology at Oxford, I was interested in animal movement, and particularly in the ways in which the characters of the animals seemed to enter their gestures—I was fascinated by the mechanics and the expressive quality of movement. When Clerk Maxwell was young, he would always ask about the "go" of things. And I've always been interested in the "go" of animals and people. Parkinsonism, for example, allows one to study "go," but as a pathological "go" —a "go" that is either haltered or driven.

And I've always had a passionate interest in the mechanisms of things: What makes a clock go? What makes the solar system go? But I've always also wondered what the inside of life is like, what it is to be a creature, to be a person? And I think that being a neurologist can bring these two interests together. Something has happened to someone's nervous system; and because of this, something has happened to someone's being.

So when something goes "wrong," so to speak, one can then examine what this reveals about the nature of being itself?

I suppose that diseases and disorders *do* provide a kind of vivisection . . . though that sounds like an awful word to use. But these are vivisections of *being,* hardly to be achieved in any other way—vivisections produced by nature in which our patients become our teachers. I think that medicine and philosophy are naturally close together, and that doctors must think philosophically and philosophers come to clinics! I regard my own work as a kind of clinical ontology.

[New York City, 1985]

Marie-Louise von Franz

FOR MANY YEARS, THE INTELLECTUAL REPUTATION AND DISCOVER-
ies of the psychologist Carl G. Jung lay hidden in the shadow cast by his
former colleague, collaborator, and coexplorer of the unconscious,
Sigmund Freud. (One is reminded of James Joyce's punning line about
being "jung and easily freudened.") Some people—many of whom had
obviously read few of his close to fifty major works—imagined Jung to
be some kind of dotty Swiss doctor who dabbled in and promulgated
occult and mystical ideas and who spent his time absorbed in theorizing
about ESP and flying saucers.

In fact, Jung was the first person to introduce and develop the concepts and notions of "individuation" (what psychologists after him were
to call "self-realization" and "self-actualization"); the "complex" (an
affectively charged group of ideas or images); "the collective unconscious" (the myth-creating aspect of the mind); the "archetypes" (the
collective universal images and motifs of myths and dreams); the terms
"extrovert/introvert" and "anima/animus" (the latter referring to the
unconscious female and male components of men's and women's personalities); the four psychological "types" (thinking, feeling, intuition,
sensation); the "active imagination" (the writing or painting of one's
unconscious fantasies and one's response to them); "synchronicity" ("A
connecting principle/Linked to the invisible/Almost imperceptible/
Something inexpressible," to quote the lines of the Police's song "Synchronicity I"); and the "Self" (the archetypal, ideal center of one's
being, about which Jung beautifully wrote: "Somewhere there was once
a Flower, a Stone, a Crystal, a Queen, a King, a Palace, a Lover, and his
Beloved, and this was long ago on an Island somewhere in the ocean
five thousand years ago. . . . Such is Love, the Mystic Flower of the
Soul. This is the Center, the Self").

With the proper understanding and help of these concepts, Jung believed, one could set out upon an interior journey, returning and bringing back to the light of consciousness the projections and shadow com-

ponents of one's unconscious life in order to create a harmony between one's inner and outer realities. Taking this journey, Jung thought, was not merely some indulgent holiday outing but a vital necessity, lest our unexamined, darker life energies lead us inescapably to a self-willed and self-destructive worldwide catastrophe. But Jung also saw that in the human psyche was a divine inner nucleus, the eternal essence of God, which could not die. And over the door of his home in Switzerland, he inscribed the ancient oracular saying: VOCATUS ATQUE NON VOCATUS DEUS ADERIT ("Called or not, the god will be there").

A recent and fascinating two-hour film titled *Matter of Heart* (made by Mark and Michael Whitney and George and Suzanne Wagner) presents interviews with twenty-one of Jung's former students, colleagues, patients, and friends—all of them in their seventies and eighties. And of these many extraordinary people, probably the most remarkable is the Swiss analyst, lecturer, and writer Marie-Louise von Franz, who was, at different periods, Jung's patient and close collaborator.

When an ancient Chinese Buddhist monk once asked his teacher whether there was any difference between the message of the Patriarchs and that of the Buddha, the teacher replied, "When you cup water in your hands, it reflects the moon; when you gather flowers, your robe absorbs the fragrance." And it is in this sense that one might well say that Marie-Louise von Franz is probably Carl Jung's most important living disciple, her work fully embodying the essence of his teachings.

But in her own right, she is an original, continually surprising, and provocative thinker, as manifested in her many astonishingly perceptive books* about such subjects as fairy tales ("They are the wisdom of cosmic matter out of which we are made"); creation myths ("The story of the origin of the world and the origin of the awareness of the world are absolutely coinciding factors"); the *puer aeternus* (the "eternal child" archetype as seen in her brilliant, path-breaking analysis of Saint-Exupéry's classic story *The Little Prince)*; alchemy (her major elaboration of

---

* Among von Franz's most important books are: *Alchemy: An Introduction to the Symbolism and the Psychology; C. G. Jung: His Myth in Our Time; Number and Time; On Divination and Synchronicity; On Dreams and Death; Patterns of Creativity Mirrored in Creation Myths; Problems of the Feminine in Fairy Tales; Projection and Re-Collection in Jungian Psychology; A Psychological Interpretation of* The Golden Ass *of Apuleius; The Problem of the Puer Aeternus; Time—Rhythm and Repose.*

One should also mention that the filmmaker and Jungian analyst Fraser Boa has produced and directed a series of twenty remarkable half-hour films entitled *The Way of the Dream,* in which Marie-Louise von Franz explains her method of dream interpretation, and goes on to analyze the dreams of scores of ordinary men and women. (This documentary series is distributed by Windrose Films Ltd., Toronto.)

Jung's notion of this subject as both a "chemical" and a "psychological" process); time (an investigation of the various and contradictory ways it has been conceived—as flux, as eternal return, and as a universal pattern of synchronous events); and projection ("If we could see through all our projections down to the last traces, our personality would be extended to cosmic dimensions").

Marie-Louise von Franz resides, practices, and writes in a book-filled house on a hilly street overlooking Lake Zurich in the town of Küsnacht, Switzerland, where Jung himself had also lived. She is a soft-spoken, commonsensible, and strong-minded person whose presence, like her work, is simultaneously challenging and healing.

The following conversation took place in the study of her home in early 1984.

*   *   *

You once mentioned that the first time you met Jung, he told you about one of his patients who felt that she had actually been on the moon.

I met Jung when I was eighteen, and at that time he told me about a vision that one of his patients had had of being on the moon, and then the man on the moon grabbed her with his black wings and didn't let her go. She was possessed by this black figure, you see. And Jung talked as if this weren't just a vision but actually as if she really *had* been on the moon. So, having a rational nature, I got irritated and said, "But she wasn't on the real moon. That was just a vision." And Jung looked at me seriously and replied, "She *was* on the moon." And I said, "Wait a minute. It can't be. She wasn't on that satellite of the planet earth, she wasn't up there." I pointed to the sky and he just looked at me again, penetratingly, and repeated, "She was on the moon." Then I got angry and thought, "Either this man's crazy or I'm stupid." And then I slowly began to realize that Jung meant that what happens psychologically is the *real* reality—I started to comprehend his concept of the reality of the psyche. And that was a big revelation.

Does this have something to do with the comment you once made that "There are indications that physical energy and psychic energy may be but two aspects of one and the same underlying reality"?

Yes, and that's really an idea that Jung developed toward the end of his life and one that I have only worked out a bit more. It's possible, for instance, that what the physicists call "energy" may in fact be the less intense frequencies of something that, in higher frequencies and at higher degrees of intensity, manifests itself as psyche. So that in the future, science may well begin to speak of only one energy that has different modes of manifestation. The brain probably transforms energies in such a way that we experience everything in a three-dimensional space. But we know from physics, too, that there are many more dimensions.

Not long ago, a medical doctor published a paper about a woman, a simple woman who woke up one morning in her hospital bed and told the nurse that she had had the following dream: She saw a candle on the windowsill that was burning down, and it began to flicker and she got terrible anxiety and felt the great darkness coming. Then there was a moment of blackout, and again she saw a light; this time, however, the candle was outside the window, the wick burning quietly. She didn't comment on it, but four hours later she died. . . . The reality, you see, was that the light went out, but in another medium, it burned on.

In one of the Gnostic Gospels, Jesus says: "If you bring forth what is within you, what you bring forth will save you. If you do not bring forth what is within you, what you do not bring forth will destroy you."

That's just it. Jung once said that you can cure a psychotic patient if you can make him creative. In other words, if what is destroying him within can be brought forth in writing or painting or some other form, then he can be cured. What we try to do is to help people bring forth the Self. That means their latent true personality or, in Gnostic terms, the God image in man. And if one creatively works that out by drawing on one's unconscious and following one's own path, then one is saved; and that very same thing undermines and destroys us if we don't do it. So that saying of Jesus is completely to the point.

I wanted to contrast this with a comment by Janet Malcolm who, writing about Freudian psychoanalysis, states: "The unexamined life may not be worth living, but the examined life is impossible to live for more than a few moments at a time. To fully accept the idea of unconscious motivation is to cease to be human. . . . To 'make the unconscious conscious' . . . is to pour water into a sieve. The moisture that remains on the surface of the mesh is the benefit of analysis."

56

That's because psychoanalytical theory is such a narrow sieve that it can't catch much of the unconscious. If you have preconceived ideas about childhood traumas and so on and don't allow for miracles, then you're going to bring up very little. Jung approached the unconscious much more openly, realizing that it's the unknown psyche, as big as the cosmos, and that we should really look at what's there. And at the end of his life he was still certain that there was more and more to discover.

In your own work, I've noticed that you tend to observe psychic events and phenomena with a very wide and open perspective. By that I mean that when you examine conflicts, you don't brush over or overlook one aspect in favor of another. In your book **Puer Aeternus,** *for instance, you suggest that the child archetype—the image of the eternal adolescent—represents charm, spontaneity, creativity, and risk-taking; but at the same time you remark that it can also reflect a destructive form of infantilism and one's entrapment in a negative mother complex. As you write: "In analysis, one tries to disentangle and definitely destroy what is really childish and [at the same time attempt to save] creativity and the future life. But practically, this is something which is immensely subtle and difficult to accomplish." How, in fact, do you go about this?*

It's very difficult to talk and make a theory about; you just have to work at it with your feeling function. Let's say, for instance, that a *puer* case comes into your office and tells you that he has a new obsession—wind surfing, say. At first you might think, "Oh Lord, another of those childish, risky sports where he'll break his neck!" But then from the tone in his voice you might suddenly have another feeling, which would tell you, "No, there's something to it. There's life and liveliness in it. It's meaningful to him." Then you get into the same conflict that he's in— now *you* are in a conflict. So you say nothing. You listen to the dreams, and then, through dream interpretation—the decisive factor is the last sentence of the dream—you deduce whether it's rather more childish or rather more constructive, and then you go with that . . . all the while holding back your own feelings that are battling within you. And in that way you allow for many more unexpected things to happen. So the word "should" should be excluded from psychology. Jung said when you use the word "should" it means you're helpless.

You've said that when a person is in a painful, unresolvable situation, he or she will often have to remain in that situation without recourse to "shoulds" or escapes or false solutions.

Yes, in order to let things happen whereby the unconscious has a say. When you're in such a situation, that's the moment that your ego must abdicate and admit, "I don't know what to do." And the analyst must also be honest enough to say, "I don't know either. But now let's look at what the unconscious psyche suggests." And then you generally find that it teaches us unexpected ways of getting out of a conflict—not directly, but in a tortuous manner. The unconscious is like a snake. Somebody comes in and tells you about a terrible conflict. And then he or she dreams about something *completely* different, as if the conflict were completely unimportant. So I just go along with that and say, "Well, let's not discuss your problem. Let's discover what the unconscious proposes. It says that you should do more painting on Saturday." "No, I have to decide whether to get a divorce or not," the patient will exclaim. And I'll say, "No, let's postpone that decision. The unconscious suggests you should do a painting." You see, it's a very good strategy, it wants to loosen up the ego and get it to be more open, and then it will clarify the issue.

You once wrote about a patient who came to see you, suffering from sexual impotence, but you treated him by analyzing his creative block instead.

I used that case to illustrate what I mean by the tortuous ways of the unconscious. That patient came with his impotence and complained that he had already tried all sorts of more direct methods—hormone injections and whatnot—and that nothing had helped. And then I said, "Let's see what your dreams say," and his dreams only talked about how his paintings weren't right and about how he should paint differently. So he said, "I've come to you for my impotence, not for that. Don't interfere with my paintings!" And I replied, "Well, I'm very sorry, but the snake makes a detour; your dreams point to something else." So I finally got him to paint differently, which released his whole emotional life; and with that, sex functioned again.

In a way, I'm reminded of that Eskimo dance drama in which one "good" and one "bad" shaman play out their magical arts against each other. First, one emerges the victor, then the other; and if one gets "killed," his adversary brings him back to life, while forgoing his own life for a moment so that both can be in balance.

Exactly. Life is a play of opposites, and thus there is never a one-sided victory. That kind of victory is a catastrophe, really, because then one of the opposites is wiped out; but it will certainly come back destructively if you don't evoke it once more. That's why Jung said you never solve a conflict, you only outgrow it. It brings you to the next level of growth, to a higher form of consciousness, and then suddenly you say, "Funny, now I have *another* conflict, that previous conflict doesn't bother me anymore."

Freud tended to see in neurosis the relics of one's unresolved past, whereas I gather that Jung thought that it contained possibilities of future growth.

Yes, Jung even spoke of the blessing of the neurosis. For him, it was a chance for growth and individual development. You see, there are two kinds of suffering. One belongs to life, which always contains a certain amount of suffering. But there's also a childish suffering that is unnecessary. If you have the wrong conscious attitude, the unconscious will work against you, and you become like the dog that tries to catch its tail and runs about in circles meaninglessly.

It sometimes seems as if an ever increasing number of people are running around in these circles.

Yes. Everybody talks about nuclear war and pollution, but our real problem is overpopulation. That's really the villain, but human beings don't like to face that. The unconscious thinks of genocide because there are too many people in the world. Before his death, Jung often said that he saw great catastrophes ahead. He had very dark forebodings. Certainly the world's situation doesn't look good. But one must give nature credit because it might invent something new, you see. At the time when Christianity came about, for instance, a wise politician in Rome would probably have had a very gloomy view about everything, too. Nine out of ten persons were slaves. The culture was at point zero, the economy was in an awful crisis. But he would certainly not have imagined that in Palestine a man would turn up who would change things with a new message. So maybe something of the kind will happen again today, and perhaps the unconscious will produce some saving movement.

59

In 1910 Jung wrote a letter to Freud in which he stated: "Only the wise are ethical from sheer intellectual presumption, the rest of us need the eternal truth of myth. . . . Two thousand years of Christianity can only be replaced by something equivalent."

Yes, that's what I was driving at. Maybe a new myth will arise in the most unexpected corner of the world. Jung always thought, for instance, that a black man would be the next Savior. So in some corner of Africa, perhaps a man will stand up and proclaim the new myth.

You've pointed out that in fairy tales, before a hero or heroine is born, there's often a period of sterility and depression during which the Queen cannot give birth. And you've talked about the idea of depression in the sense of the ego pressing down *into the unconscious.*

Depression can be a very salutary thing, if one knows how to handle it. I myself was terribly depressed when I first went into Jungian analysis. I complained about it, and Jung just smiled and said, "Well, 'depression' comes from the Latin word *deprimere,* so if you're sad, just sit down and go into your sadness until something comes up from it. If you're depressed, you're too high up in your mind." And sometimes I'd sit for a whole afternoon just staring ahead of me. And then suddenly I had fantasies. Jung encouraged me to write them down, and the creative flow began.

You've written a wonderful book about creation myths that is, in fact, about the creative process itself. And in that book you state that the many stories of the origins of the universe and the origins of our awareness *of the universe are absolutely coinciding factors. That's a fascinating and certainly a true idea, since we don't really know what happened before the beginning of creation.*

The only thing we can describe is when we woke up to our awareness of the universe. And that's the moment when it became real. There are thousands of creation myths, and they're all variations and different facets of this basic process.

You write about myths that conceive of a creation-from-above or a creation-from-below, which reminds me of the Greek philosopher Heraclitus' statement that "The way up and the way down are one and the same."

Absolutely. Only when it comes from the below you have the experience that a creative idea or painting or whatever you are doing comes out of your belly. And when it comes from above, it seems as if it drops from the sky into your head—it's inspired from above, so to speak. But these are only qualitatively different feelings, they're the same thing, really.

You've asserted that "Where there is a creative constellation in the unconscious, that is, when the unconscious has conceived a child, if we do not put it out in the form of creative work, we get possessed by it instead."

People get absolutely intolerable when they have a creative idea in their womb and can't bring it out. They're neurotic, aggressive, irritable, and depressed. So then one has to help them bring the child out.

You've also said that "Every step forward toward building up more consciousness destroys a previous living balance."

I had in mind the fact that medieval man, in spite of all the horrors of the times, was at home in an explained world. He was contained in the revealed truth of the Catholic Church; and even if he was against it, he still believed in it. The birth of science, however, made man a homeless wanderer. It was necessary, it was a kind of progress, but it destroyed something.

You once pointed out that among the Australian aborigines, when the rice crop shows signs of failure, the women go into the rice field, bend down, and tell the grains of rice the story of their origins.

We have to have a conception of where we come from and where we are going—a wider conception—and then we can be at home in the world. And that's why historical and mythological knowledge is so important. In *The Book of Enoch* we read how angels had intercourse with human women and created giants. The angels taught the giants about magic, natural sciences, and technology, and then they nearly destroyed the earth. For this was a too rapid invasion of new creative contents into the conscious world, and people suffered from inflated notions and ideas. Just like today. I recently read, for example, that soon we'll be putting electrodes into the brains of children so that they can learn better in school. Imagine that inflated idea!

I don't know. If someone told me that with those electrodes implanted in me I'd be able to speak any language in the world, I might be tempted!

If that were possible. But there would undoubtedly be drawbacks. You might be able to speak, but your memory might not be able to store things. Or maybe, suddenly one day, you'd develop terrible headaches and all sorts of side effects. You can see how with modern medicines people die from these effects. The medical world doesn't save more people nowadays than it did before.

You once wrote that when the ego identifies with the Self and begins to think, "I've got the message! I've got the true meaning!" one winds up with pathological demagogues and pseudo prophets. You mention Hitler, Charles Manson, and others as examples, stating, "They have inflicted infinite damage on the world because they have transformed normal inner experiences of the unconscious into morbid poison through inflated identification with them."

I think it's indisputable that Hitler was destructive, and Charles Manson, too. One step further and you'd meet them in the lunatic asylums. In the asylums you have a lot of so-called gifted people who have invented the *perpetuum mobile* and answered the world riddles and so on. I sometimes get letters from inhabitants of such clinics. They always have *the* great idea, but when you look at it it's completely hazy, completely fuzzy. They haven't worked it out.

There are some young people who identify with the unconscious and fall into the world of dreams and neglect to build up their actual personal lives, while some others believe that with terrorism they can change the world. But you can never do that without the help of the unconscious. You have to keep your critical mind intact, you can't just be naïve with the unconscious. That's why, for instance, in shamanism the young apprentice always needs a teacher, because if he stepped into the ghost world alone, he would fall for all sorts of traps. The unconscious doesn't want to trap us, it's not wicked. But it *is* difficult to deal with, and it's sometimes very hard to find out what it really wants to say.

You've made a connection between the psychotherapist and the shaman, and have said that a shaman has to have been wounded in order for him to heal. Since you're a therapist, perhaps you were wounded, too.

In my childhood I hated my mother and didn't get on with her. Perhaps she wasn't as bad as I thought, but she was extremely different from me, a very powerful person who wanted to make me what she thought I should be. She was a smashing extrovert and I'm a deep introvert. So that was part of my problem when I met Jung. And if I hadn't had depressions and that difficulty with my mother, I probably wouldn't have gone into Jungian psychology and learned about the unconscious, which released my creativity and which enabled me to help other people. If it hadn't been for the trouble with my mother, I would probably just have done what she wanted me to do, which was to marry a rich man and have children.

You've said that "People who don't know much about Jungian psychology think it is something esoteric and aristocratic. They don't realize that the process moves in two directions: a) becoming more individual and less identical with the emotions, and moving upward to greater differentiation; but also b) integrating the man in the street."

Yes. And that's why Jung could talk to anybody, even to half-wits. They adored him, and he gave them analytical hours. Once, for instance, a parson sent him a farmer's girl from a mountain village. She couldn't sleep, she hadn't slept for a whole year, and even pills hadn't helped. And when she turned up in his office, Jung saw at once that she was a half-wit and completely uneducated, and he couldn't do any therapy with her. So he took her on his knees and rocked her and sang her lullabies. And from then on, she slept. When the parson wrote to Jung asking, "How did you cure her?" Jung replied, "I couldn't talk to her, so I sang her some lullabies." And the parson was furious because he thought Jung was lying!

You see, we still have Stone Age people and we have medieval people, and it's much better that they get cured in a style appropriate to them. I once, for instance, sent a patient to an exorcist. And if someone goes to a voodoo doctor in Haiti, it may very well help. Certain people are on that level, and they need to be cured on that level.

Recently, both Jung and Freud have come under attack for their so-called sexual adventures or misadventures—as if these somehow negated all their theories and teachings.

It's so naïve that I can only laugh at it. And since Freud taught that one shouldn't repress sexuality, then he shouldn't have repressed his sexuality either. And for the same reason I always smile when Freudians attack Jung over the Spielrein affair [Sabina Spielrein, one of Jung's first patients, was cured by Jung and became his lover].

Jung and Freud had theoretical differences. Their disagreement wasn't only a personal affair. Not at all. And now Jung is becoming more and more known. I mean, the number of Jungian analysts increases every year, the interest in Jung increases, the sales of his books increase—everything increases—and so, naturally, the opposition increases, too. For a while I noticed the Freudians were no longer against Jung. They thought he was passé, finished. So they weren't aggressive anymore about him. But now that terrible snake is raising its head again, to speak their language, so one has to stamp it out. But young people are discovering Jung all over the world. I get a lot of letters from sixteen- and seventeen-year-olds who have begun to read Jung or my work, and they want to know more about it.

Freud, you know, was terrified of the flood of occultism, his attitude being that one should not provoke it. And it is true that nowadays there is a certain turning toward the unconscious, with the misuse of drugs, that is thoroughly unhealthy. Many people also sit absolutely dazed in front of the TV for hours and hours—and that's a kind of falling into the unconscious. But we need the unconscious. It's only a question of dealing with it in a healthy manner, though there will always be a certain number of individuals who'll do it the wrong way.

You've said that the first dream that one recalls from one's childhood "often sets forth in symbolic form the essence of an entire life or of the first part of life. It reflects, so to speak, a piece of the 'inner fate' into which the individual was born." And when I've asked friends of mine to recount their first remembered dreams, they've always been extraordinary.

They *are* amazing. You should read the four volumes of seminars that Jung gave on such dreams that adults remember from their childhood, and also a few dreams that little children have told their parents. Jung interprets them. And they're fascinating.

I remember one dream he talks about in which a little girl saw herself lying in her bed and Jack Frost came in and pinched her in the belly. And Jung interpreted that as being most dangerous because the girl had no reaction when the demon of cold and winter was pinching her in the seat of emotions, the fire center. And do you know what happened? She eventually became schizophrenic, took a pistol, and shot herself in the belly. That's how she died. She executed herself. The cold hand of death. So there was a bit of fate anticipated already in the childhood dream. A bad one in that case. . . . The first dreams—one should make many more studies about them.

What about the idea of synchronicity? The recent rock and roll album by the Police is deeply involved with that idea.

I think it's one of Jung's key concepts, and one that will have great importance in the future. As you know, synchronicity is the simple coincidence of two factors that are connected, not causally but rather through meaning. Have you heard about the Einstein-Podolsky-Rosen paradox in physics? To put it in simple words is very difficult, but let's say you have two particles that have once been connected but are then separated. And let's say one is in New York City and the other is in Tokyo. Now, at the moment you alter the spin of the one in New York, the spin of the other in Tokyo appears altered, too—so quickly that even a light signal couldn't have been exchanged. In other words, one particle knows what the other one, thousands of kilometers away, is doing. This reveals the so-called inseparability of the universe. The same is true in psychology.

The ancient Chinese said that a person sitting alone in his room think-ing the right thoughts will be heard a thousand miles away.

Yes. Confucius said that, and that is synchronicity. Everything is con-tained in the oneness such that everything is connected with everything else in a meaningful way. And the physicists are actually getting at it now from their angle.

Jung and you often refer to the fourfold structure of the psyche, and to the fact that each person contains an anima and an animus.

Yes. There's the feminine nature in man and the masculine nature in woman, so there are four of us in this room right now. And that four-fold structure—you find it in basic physical theories, in myths, in fairy tales, and endlessly in dreams and in art. I mean, think of all those fourfold mandalas and pyramids.

Why four?

I think that's a just-so story that we can't explain. The meaning of *one* has to do with the spiritual oneness of everything. *Two* has to do with polarity—yin and yang. *Three* generally is concerned with dynamic movement and processes, such that in fairy tales you read about three giants or coming upon three rivers. And with *four,* you arrive at completion: One, two, three, *four.* And that gives the feeling of complete reality.

Jung's formulation of the four functional "types"—thinking, feeling, intuition, sensation—has been criticized as fairly naïve and reductive, but it seems to make sense to me as a way of seeing certain strengths and weaknesses in a person.

Practically, I use them all the time. For me they're the great peacemaking instrument, because you can settle hundreds of quarrels by telling someone: "Now look here, you're a sensation type and have no fantasy, while your friend's an intuitive type and has no sensation, and that's why you clashed." You can always make peace between people by revealing that to them. A lot of friction and marriage troubles and troubles in offices are in fact typological misunderstandings.

Jung also posited the notion of "active imagination." What is that?

You have it out with a fantasy. Let's say you do a painting of a black fox; then you hang it over your bed and you talk to it and say, "Black fox, why have you come to me? What's your message?" And then you listen to what it says. This is a two-way process, not only to let it out as fantasy but then to let it in again by integration.

What about the notion of the "complex"?

Jung discovered the "complex," by which he meant a cluster of emotionally tuned representations generally surrounding an archetypal kernel. Quite simply, if you have a money complex, then with anything that has to do with money, you get emotional—people begin to tremble when they have to take change out of their pockets, for example. Or there's the inferiority complex. That's another one. There are many complexes. What is interesting is that whenever something touches the complex, people get cold or sweaty hands, say. There's a psychic *and* physiological reaction to it. And if you want to find out what complexes a person has, all you have to do is just remain absolutely silent and let the other person talk and talk and talk and you'll always end up with the complex. If you make an empty space, the complex walks in.

You yourself have dealt with subjects as diverse as alchemy, fairy tales, time, and number. I assume that your classical education made that possible.

When I was young, I didn't know what I should study. I hesitated between mathematics, medicine, and classical languages. And then one night I dreamt that I was sitting on the Acropolis as a wanderer, with no money and a knapsack between my knees. The sun was shining, and suddenly, from the right, all the Olympic gods entered in a big procession, and they begged—they stretched out their hands begging. I opened my sack and wanted to give them something, but I had nothing except a loaf of bread. So I cut the loaf into bits, and I gave every god a piece, apologizing and saying, "I'm very sorry, but that's all I have." And after that, I decided to study classical languages, because the gods wanted something from me.

What gods appeared to you?

All of them—Zeus and Hera and Hermes and Aphrodite. The whole bunch.

Which one do you feel most connected to now?

I've changed. It used to be Hermes. Now I'm interested in Aphrodite.

A very jealous goddess!

Yes. That's one of her less good traits. But she also has sublime love and erotic love, she has a whole scale and range. For me, now, this goddess has become dominant. There are no "shoulds" about it. I just try to follow the stream of life, and where there's the most life and energy, that's where I try to be.

[Küsnacht, Switzerland, 1984]

67

Federico Fellini

ONE SUNNY MORNING, WHEN HE WAS NINE YEARS OLD, FILM-maker Federico Fellini ran away from his religious boarding school in Fano, Italy. Next to the market in the town square was a small circus. As Fellini remembers it, he went into an empty tent, breathed in the odor of sawdust, noticed the hanging trapezes, and then caught sight of "a fat girl with beautiful plump bare legs who was sewing spangles on a tutu." Hearing a moan, the young Federico followed the sound to another tent. "And I saw before me a scene from the Nativity," Fellini writes in a memoir. "A zebra was stretched out on the ground. And around the zebra was, first, an old man, wearing the great collar of the clown, whose face bore the marks of deepest despair; then there was an old lady who was whimpering, and three or four children . . . all in a state of suspense and tender solicitude toward the animal. While I was standing there, fascinated by the sight, I felt myself violently shoved aside, and I saw a man enter carrying a valise, who was revealed to be the veterinarian."

The veterinarian discovered that the zebra had eaten a chocolate bar that had made it sick, and he asked that someone bring a pail of water to the ailing animal. Federico quickly did so, and the zebra eventually revived. "Finally, two hours later," Fellini recalls, "I found myself sitting in their caravan; they fed me, gave me a slice of sausage, and nobody asked me who I was. Then, at twilight, they began to play music; they put on their costumes. I saw the girl with the beautiful thick legs; she had put on a skintight costume that had a lot of feathers. . . . I felt I had come home at last. But then, just as the performance was about to begin, the old clown, who was called Pierino, said to me: 'But what are you doing here? Who are you?' So I said to him, 'Me, I'm the one who went to get water for the zebra,' and he answered, 'Ah, yes, that's right, that's right,' and he kept me beside him, like a father. Then I saw him go into the ring to perform his number; he made me laugh and cry a lot. . . . I was truly exalted. Nobody asked me anything."

Ever since making such extraordinary films as *I Vitelloni, La Strada, Nights of Cabiria, La Dolce Vita, 8½,* and *Amarcord,* Federico Fellini has been habitually asked questions about the meanings of the characters and images in his work, the seeds of which are easily discovered in the director's early memory of his deeply dreamlike encounter with the circus in Fano.

It has been suggested that dream interpretation arises when we have lost touch with our inner nighttime images, when we no longer experience them as fully real. In the same sense, Fellini has always insisted that we observe the images in his films, not with cultural preconceptions and theoretical biases, but with the innocent eyes of children. And, as he once said, "It is necessary to understand childhood as the possibility of maintaining an equilibrium between the unconscious and the conscious, between 'real' life and the life of memory." It is in this light that one recalls the images of the deserted piazza at night in *I Vitelloni,* the sea at dawn at the end of *La Dolce Vita,* the holy Fool in *La Strada* grieving over his broken watch, the heroine of *Nights of Cabiria* wandering alone through the forest, and the peacock in *Amarcord* opening out its wings in falling snow . . . and one is reminded of psychologist James Hillman's remark that "Dreams call from the imagination to the imagination and can be answered only by the imagination."

In his most beautiful and imaginative film since *Amarcord,* Fellini's *And the Ship Sails On* takes place in 1914 on the eve of World War I, as opera singers, impresarios, aristocratic guests, a group of Serbian refugees, and a lovesick rhinoceros (perhaps an unconscious remembrance of the sick circus zebra of Fellini's childhood) find themselves together on a luxury liner that sets out to fulfill the last wish of a world-renowned diva by scattering her ashes over the Adriatic. Opening with haunting black-and-white silent-movie images that slowly transform themselves into sepia and dreamlike colors, *And the Ship Sails On* was filmed entirely at Cinecittà—the famous Roman film studios that are a veritable dream factory—in which Fellini has created a magical, "unreal" world (the sea is made of cellophane and the moon of paper) that seems more real than reality itself.

The following interview took place in February 1984 in the director's office in Rome. Hanging on the walls one saw a Moebius strip, Indian paintings, a photograph of Carl Jung, and three Tarot cards (Strength, the Stars, the Fool). And in one corner of the room, resting on a small table, were a small Buddha and a marionette—a microcosm of the Fellinian world.

*   *   *

In thinking about your first encounter with the circus, I was moved and struck by the sense you had of "coming home at last."

When you're a child, there's a possibility of foreseeing what your future life will actually be, of recognizing an atmosphere and a dimension that, mysteriously, somehow seem very familiar to you. So when a child who will later become a priest first steps into a church, he will be overwhelmed by the attraction he feels there. I only remember the coldness and gloominess I experienced being in church, but when I discovered that circus, I had the impression of something that seemed more familiar to me than school, even than my own family. So now, when I think back on that moment, I see that it must have been some kind of announcement. It's very strange that a nine-year-old boy stepping into a circus should feel so protected and invaded by such a warmth. Circus people are never very surprised by things that happen to them. I was a child and they—in particular, the clown Pierino, who was the boss of that circus—simply accepted me. I really felt that I was in the center of a town that was my town. And it was the same feeling I had many years later when I went to Cinecittà.

Clowns and children seem to understand each other—fools to some, Fools to others.

A fool is someone who has lost his rationality, lost a part of himself. To be consciously a Fool, however—that is the great challenge, the great realization. But I feel a little bit stupid saying things like that, so I would prefer that we talked about movies. About my job.

"Roll away the reel world, the reel world, the reel world!"

Who wrote that?

James Joyce.

It's a very appropriate pun. Somebody once said that no one is more realistic than the person who has visions because he intensifies the most

profound reality, which is his reality. The expression of the visionary—
the painter or director—is a translation of his vision. And the result of
this operation is absolute reality.

*Certain people have criticized you for having given up the neorealistic
vision of* La Strada *and* Nights of Cabiria *in favor of the vision of
artifice that one finds in your new film* And the Ship Sails On, *in
which the sea is made out of cellophane and the moon out of paper.*

This is a very silly accusation. First of all, I don't see the difference
between neorealism and artifice. But even if one accepted these kind of
statements, it would be like accusing a person of having gone from the
age of twenty to the age of forty. It's just a path that you have to follow.
What people call artifice is the only way I can express my interior reality. It's like accusing an artist who paints a picture of a field of working
with colors instead of using the real grass.

Thoreau once said, "Our truest life is when we are in dreams awake."

Yes, in a certain sense, though ultimately I think I disagree with this.
Because very often in a dream you're not really aware of what is happening. It would be more appropriate to be able to live as if you were
watching yourself live—becoming more aware of what is going on. In
the dream, however, this kind of awareness is lacking, even if it may be
the intention of the dream to tell you through symbols what is happening to you, in order to get you to be a bit more detached from your
emotions, while representing them to you as if you were watching a
movie. Because it's true that talking about dreams is like talking about
movies, since the cinema uses the language of dreams: years can pass in
a second and you can hop from one place to another. It's a language
made of image. And in the real cinema, every object and every light
means something, as in a dream.

And that's why television has killed movies—it has wounded the cinema in its most precious part. Because it uses the language of film, but
in a different context, and it reduces its proportions. So you don't have
the same impression of sleep that you get when you step into a movie
theater—that solemn, almost religious ritual of stepping into the realm
of visions, as when you go to sleep and start to dream . . . like stepping into the cinema and suddenly the lights go off and you start watching this enormous screen. Television, on the other hand, constantly
projects images through that little box; and while watching TV, people

chat, eat, etc. It's as if you were dreaming by being awake, but in such a way you actually can pay no attention to your dream because you're awake. And in that way, TV has killed the heart of the movies.

You once commented: "Going to the cinema is like returning to the womb. You sit there still and meditative in the darkness, waiting for life to appear on the screen. One should go to the cinema with the innocence of a fetus."

Maybe my mother, when I was a fetus, brought me to the cinema. I don't remember [laughing]. But what I meant is that I think an audience should see a picture without any kind of bombardment of advice or interpretation. When I speak of the innocence of the spectator, I'm thinking of someone who goes into the theater because he's attracted by the poster. He doesn't know who did the movie, he just looks—and here we are again—like a dreamer. If a dreamer was warned beforehand that what he was about to dream meant this or that—the black horse means this, the blood that—he wouldn't go to bed because he wouldn't want to dream anymore. It often happens that the spectator is scared off by knowing that he has to see a movie by Ingmar Bergman or Luis Buñuel. And when he sits there, trying to think what they're trying to say, he doesn't see the film.

What was the first film that you remember seeing? And what was the first that gave you a feeling that you wanted to be a director?

The first film that I saw—I was seven years old and I didn't imagine it could concern me in any way—was called *Masciste Inferno*. Masciste was someone like Hercules—a character taken from a poem by Gabriele D'Annunzio—a very strong, almost-naked man who was in hell. And I remember that the movie theater was very crowded and outside it was raining, so most of the people were standing up in wet coats. I remember smelling all that wet cloth. It was a silent movie, a little man was under the screen playing the piano, and I was on the arm of my father. It was the first time I saw these big shadows moving. The room was full of cigarette smoke that passed through the ray of light, and I was much more interested in watching the smoke and the movement and all the curls that it made in the light than in the film itself. But I was affected and touched by a big woman—it was Proserpina, the Queen of Hell, with big fat eyes, big breasts, and very made up like a singer. She made a sudden gesture, and suddenly there was a circle of flames all around

Masciste. And probably this image of that strong, beautiful woman—
like a big, regal, royal whore—must have struck me because I always
put her into all my films after that.

Watching movies, I never thought that I was going to be a director. I
knew that I wasn't going to be a lawyer, an engineer, or a doctor as my
mother would have liked. But I never imagined that I would become a
director. I knew in a sort of vague and confused way that I would like to
be an actor or a puppet master or a painter or a sculptor—an artist of
some sort. Because when I was in Rimini as a child, I saw that the artists
—who were painters and sculptors on the whole—were looked upon
with both diffidence—a sort of moralist judgment—and envy at the
same time. Anyway, they were considered different from everyone else,
and so I was particularly attracted to these characters. They dressed in a
different way, they had big ties, they didn't go to school, they had
models coming around, they ate at hours no one else did—they had this
freedom of life, and they were always spending time together. My father, and especially my mother, used to speak very badly of them, and
that, of course, made them very likable. These people with long hair
and beards were more familiar to me than my own family; when I was
with them, I felt the same way as I had felt at the circus. And from the
age of ten or eleven, I began going into the artists' ateliers and played
with colors and made little sculptures.

So when I finished school, I thought I'd be a journalist or a writer or
an actor. And eventually I managed to find my work, which united all
these things together. Because in my job you can be a bit of a journalist,
a bit of a painter, a bit of a puppet master, an actor—you're a bit of
everything. In fact, I started as a screenplay writer, and sometimes I was
called into the studio to correct or add some dialogue. But I always
entered the studio with an uneasy feeling, because the crowd, the
screaming, all that confusion made me very unhappy. So I never
thought I could be a movie director.

But it happened, and in a very spontaneous way, without thinking
that that was to be my real life. I just started to help a friend of mine, for
whom I wrote a screenplay called *Closed Shutters*. It was the first time
that he had the job of director, and he had a breakdown—Monday,
Tuesday, Wednesday, Thursday . . . he couldn't work. He was over-
come by anxiety and the anguish of being responsible for a hundred
persons. The producer insisted that I try to give him some confidence.
So I went to Turin, where he was supposed to be shooting, and saw and
felt that this poor man was totally impotent. I tried to help him and
spent hours talking to him. Then we went together for the first day on

the set, and it was very difficult because my friend had to film a scene—that I had written!—in which someone had drowned in the river. There were all these people on the beach, and the police were arriving with their boats. And I saw that my friend was desperate on the set. So I took the loudspeaker and ordered the camera to move here and there. I was doing the job for someone else, so I was extremely relaxed and natural about it. And probably, at that moment, the spirit of the director emerged from inside me. And I became a director by doing exactly all those things that used to bother me: I was arrogant, yelling, insulting, commanding, treating actors badly, having houses moved, telling the sun to move a little bit further down! And I directed until evening. The producer obviously wanted me to go on, but since I didn't want to hurt my friend, another director came and took his place. At that moment, however, I understood that I was able to direct. And maybe, in a few years time, when I become completely incompetent, the producer will call *another* director to help me, and then *he* will start directing, and the chain will go on. Maybe.

Aside from the circus and the artists of Rimini, what else influenced you creatively as a child?

Fairy tales. My grandmother used to tell them to me. She was a farmer, a peasant, and her stories—since she lived in the country and was surrounded by animals—always concerned horses, cats, owls, bats. So we grew up to respect and be very curious about them. And still today, when I eat a chicken, I'm afraid that suddenly it will become a prince once it's inside me! [laughing] I've always had—and still have—this feeling.

Also, when I was eight or nine, *Pinocchio* was an enormous influence. It isn't just a wonderful book, for me it's one of the great books—equal to *The Odyssey* and Franz Kafka's *The Trial*. And for my generation, it was our first happy encounter with the object of a book. Because when you're small, a book is something very strange that belongs to the world of adults—something that has to do with school, something that takes away your freedom—unless there are beautiful pictures inside. And mostly it was something you could throw at your brother when you were fighting [laughing]. But ultimately, it was something that didn't belong to you. The encounter with *Pinocchio* was like coming upon a magical object—it was a big bridge between life and culture—so it had special meaning, almost exorcistic.

Now the author, Collodi, lived in the nineteenth century, so he had to conclude the book in a certain moralistic way. And it ends with the transformation of the puppet into a boy. That, however, is the least interesting, and even the saddest, part of the book. But of course it's true that we all lose the magical, childhood, Pinocchio part of our being —being in touch with animals, with the night, with mystery . . . contacting with life the way it should be. And with this loss, we become good idiots, good students, good husbands, good citizens.

Pinocchio is a marvelous book beause you can read it forever—when you're a child, when you're young, when you're old. It has the simplicity of the Bible and lacks all presumptuous consciousness. And, indeed, it really is a work of magic. You can open it like a book of oracles, read just one line, and it will help you—all your doubts and problems find an answer on those pages.

The novelist Italo Calvino has written: "You reach a moment in life when, among the people you have known, the dead outnumber the living. And the mind refuses to accept more faces, more expressions: on every new face you encounter, it prints the old forms, for each one it finds the most suitable masks." Is this true for you when you look for the "faces" of your new films?

When a character is born in your imagination, it has a certain function in the story that you want to tell, and the face has to express this character. So you tend to look for one that can immediately suggest to the spectator who this person is. I don't tell psychological stories—stories in which characters develop throughout the film—so the character has to declare himself right from the start. For that reason, I try to find faces that are immediately believable and fascinating. And that is the reason why, when making a picture, I spend most of my time in testing, in order to discover the right facial materialization and incarnation of the role—an expressive mask. And of all the phases of the preparation, choosing the faces is perhaps the most anxious and even dramatic one, because what you're looking for is in your mind.

I'll try, for example, to represent on a piece of paper with pen and ink and colors the kind of faces I imagine. I'll think of, say, the captain of the boat in *And the Ship Sails On.* I'll make a sketch at my desk, then people will start coming into my office. And the fact that someone is there, alive, with a real voice, with a particular slight accent . . . the fact that he's smoking, that I see his hands, his flesh, suggests to me that, even if he isn't right for the part, even if he's exactly the opposite of what I'm looking for, the fact that he's alive creates a very strong temptation for me. I say to myself, "What I have in mind is just a sketch, a phantom, but here is a real creature." But then another person appears, completely different. "So why not?" I say. "Maybe this is the one." And then comes another, and another.

So to try to be faithful to what you had in mind and not to refuse any new suggestions that life gives you is sometimes very difficult. For that reason, I have a folder into which I put many different photographic solutions for each character: One actor is little, another tall, another fat, another thin, another has a nice face, another is ugly. Sometimes an actor seems right by himself, but not when put together with someone else. The captain's face might be good for one century, but the face of the second officer might be the face of two centuries before—so they can't stay together. This kind of dialectical joke sometimes makes me feel lost, and my ship may have fifteen or twenty captains. But, finally, I have to decide. And at that moment, I have confidence that my labyrinthine research will have paid off.

For instance, I started *And the Ship Sails On* without having chosen all the characters. Even during the third week of shooting, I hadn't cast the blind Austro-Hungarian princess, and the production was going crazy because the day of the first scene with the princess was coming up, and I still didn't know who it was going to be. It's like landing an airplane when you can't see any sign of an airport. But I always have confidence, even when everybody around me gets crazy. But two nights before the shooting of the first scene with the blind princess, I was still feeling very unsure and lost, because I didn't know where to find a blind princess of an empire that no longer existed. But then that night, a friend of mine took me to see the dance company of Pina Bausch, a German choreographer, who had come to perform for the first time in Rome. Usually, I don't go to the dance or ballet—I feel a little bit foreign to that. But I went to see this show, it was excellent, and afterward we went backstage to say hello to her. And as I walked into the dressing room, there was the blind princess who was waiting for me with a pale face and a detached, cruel smile—someone who was a cross between a saint and a madwoman. So, this is just to say that if you really put yourself honestly and sincerely, with childish enthusiasm, into the trip or voyage, things will always come to you.

There's an old text from India that gives three rules for the theater: 1) That it must be encouraging and amusing to the drunk; 2) That it must respond to someone who asks, "How to live?"; and 3) That it answer the one who asks, "How does the universe work?" What do you think?

I'm not Indian; I was born in Rimini [laughing]. So I have a completely different . . . well, not completely different, but a slightly different attitude to this. First, I don't think a drunk needs to go to the theater or the movies, because once he's drunk, he sees everything he wants to anyway. So when I'm working, I don't have the thought of making a picture for a drunk. . . . I don't know, I'll think about it.

You know, I've sometimes been accused of not thinking enough about the audience. But I find that a really goofy and strange accusation. For if one pretends to be a person who can speak and tell stories to someone else . . . if one believes in and has chosen the profession of a storyteller, then it's clear that inside of oneself there must be this sort of push, this drive to be clear to others. But apart from that, it's impossible for me to try consciously, practically, technically to make a film for an audience. You don't know who that is, and it's a silly pretension. If you have a restaurant, you naturally can think of the various tastes of the people who come. But if you intend to make culture or express your fantasies, then you can't expect to think of an audience. The only thing you have to be faithful and loyal to is to the characters of the story: you have to obey them. The characters are the real audience to which one must pay attention. And if you can satisfy their demands, then you have created the proper ground for the audience to receive and understand them. But if you have to think of a particular audience—and an audience of drunks—never!

Now, as far as thinking of satisfying someone who wants to know how the universe works, I can't imagine why a person would go to a movie expecting that kind of explanation.

In And the Ship Sails On, *I thought I found out a little bit about how the universe works—what with the cosmic music played by several passengers on the ship's kitchen glasses and the mantric* om *intoned by the basso profundo who hypnotizes a chicken.*

You did?

Maybe I was drunk.

Maybe [laughing]. But I didn't have that in mind when I made the movie. And as far as answering the question "How to live?"—if a work of art is honest and sincere and expresses loyally the problems, emotions, and experiences of the author's life, then it will always have something in it that concerns and affects the person in the audience who is looking to find some point in common.

When once asked, "What is requisite for an entertainer?" you replied: "A mixture of magician and prestidigitator, of prophet and clown, of tie salesman and priest who preaches."

That's true. I think that someone who pretends to be a storyteller has to be a prophet, clown, trickster, and magician. A creative person—let's say that awful word: an artist—makes what we call magical operations. Because if something lives only in his imagination, totally hidden to others, then people won't be able to imagine it. So, with his talent, experience, artisanal sense, materials and colors, an artist makes things visible for everybody, like the magician in a fairy tale who makes something that wasn't there suddenly appear. Because the artist always lives somewhere in between the unconscious and the prevailing cultural standards, and he attempts to combine the two. Or one could refer to the twilight zone between the sun and the moon, which is the same borderline between what is unconscious and what is real. And so the artist is particularly moved by the light that is between—between two attitudes, two sets of behavior, two dimensions. He is moved by the twilight because then one finds the union of contrasts. And the ground on which the artist stands and works is also like that of the magician who operates on what doesn't exist—or just confusedly exists—and turns it into something concrete and ordered.

Do you think there's a connection here between the magician and the tribal shaman and medicine man who, through the overcoming of their own psychic wounds, are able to heal others?

You could say that the process of creativity is, in a certain sense, a kind of sickness or illness. You're invaded by a germ, something that has to grow inside you and that makes you completely sick; and the therapy is to materialize the germ of the fantasy so that you become cured. And it's possible that what you've done can turn out to be therapeutic for other people.

In And the Ship Sails On *when you show everyone—the Serbian refugees and the upper classes—dancing together on the lower deck, I felt a kind of curative power at work.*

81

You know, when I make a picture, I want to tell a story. And I'm glad and sometimes even a little bit surprised by different interpretations and points of view. But I feel a little bit ridiculous encouraging this kind of approach to my films. What you said now about the dance may be true. But for me, the important thing about a creation is whether it's alive or not. I don't care about aesthetical, philosophical, or ideological points of view. But if I had to say something about the dance you referred to, I'd say it's simply a moment of drunkenness, of pure and innocent energy that breaks down the barriers and defenses between the bourgeoisie and the slaves. All that detachment and distance is transcended by means of music. It's a moment of life that suggests that things could be better if we broke through our defenses and egotism.

But, basically, I don't like to say stupid things about what is done. Do, don't talk. And do it while being awake—even if sleepily awake—and, as the ancient Chinese used to say, "intentionally without intention."

[Rome, 1984]

George Balanchine

GEORGE BALANCHINE (1904–83) WAS GENERALLY CONSIDERED TO be the greatest choreographer of modern times. He studied music and dance in St. Petersburg and made his dancing debut at the age of ten as a cupid in the Maryinsky Theatre Ballet Company production of *The Sleeping Beauty*. He later served as ballet master for Serge Diaghilev's famous *Ballets Russes de Monte Carlo*. At the end of 1933, he traveled to the United States, where, along with the distinguished dance connoisseur and man-of-letters Lincoln Kirstein, he helped to found both the School of American Ballet and the New York City Ballet, of which he was the artistic director.

For this continually inspiring company, Balanchine created scores of masterpieces, including *Serenade*, *The Four Temperaments*, *Jewels*, *A Midsummer Night's Dream*, and *Vienna Waltzes*, whose "dance evolutions and figures"—in the words of the late poet and critic Edwin Denby—were "luminous in their spacing, and of a miraculous musicality in their impetus." Among the greatest of his works were his more than thirty ballets to the scores of Igor Stravinsky, with whom he was associated since 1925, when he choreographed a revised version of the composer's *The Song of the Nightingale*. In the collaborations between these two Russian masters, one became ineluctably conscious of "seeing" music and "hearing" movements, as music and dance revealed sound and light to be two manifestations of one vibrational source.

*　*　*

I was fortunate enough to meet with and interview George Balanchine on two occasions. The first time was in July of 1978 at the opening of the New York City Ballet's annual summer season in Saratoga Springs, New York. The second time occurred exactly four years later in July of 1982, during one of the final performances of the City Ballet's Stravinsky Centennial Celebration, held during that month. It was to be Balanchine's final interview. Several months later he entered New York

City's Roosevelt Hospital, suffering from progressive cerebral disintegration. He died on April 30, 1983.

Mr. B. (as Balanchine was known to his colleagues) held at bay almost all kinds of visionary and speculative theorizing about his work, preferring to talk about himself as a craftsman rather than a creator, and comparing himself to a cook and a cabinetmaker (he was apparently extremely adept at both endeavors) and even, as he did once with me, to a horse!

Both of my conversations with George Balanchine concerned themselves with music. As the composer George Perle writes in his liner notes to the marvelous *A Balanchine Album* (Nonesuch Records): "Balanchine was an accomplished musician, but he was much more than this. Just as the words of a Schubert *Lied* have become Schubert's words, whoever the poet may have been, so the music of a Balanchine ballet becomes Balanchine's composition, not because he has appropriated it, but because he seems to have magically reexperienced the creative act, to have relived the decisions, the choices, and eliminations that the composer has lived through in bringing it into being."

Witty, gracious, childlike, and charming, Balanchine conversed with me, both in 1978 and 1982, in his inimitable, idiosyncratically flavored English. During our second conversation, I noticed that Balanchine's mind would occasionally wander, and that he would respond to one question with the answer to another. When asked about Stravinsky's childhood, for example, he proceeded to talk about his own. But as the following two interviews both make clear, Balanchine always refused to dwell on the past or the future. ("I'm not interested in later on. I don't have any later on. We all live in the same time forever.") And the only way to pay tribute to the spirit of this twentieth-century genius is simply to regard his ballets as eternally new creations.

*   *   *

Of all the art forms, music and dance seem to be the closest—like brother and sister, or like lovers. And whenever I think of your ballets, I hear the dancers and see the music.

Anything that doesn't belong to the world of words, you can't explain. People say, "What do you feel when you look at this?" We always have to compare with something else. "Is it beautiful?" "Yes." "Well, how beautiful?" "Like a rose, like a taste, like a wine." "And what does wine taste like?" "Like grass." It's always something else. So you describe my ballets in terms of hearing; and you're a writer, so you write. I myself don't have a writing style . . . not at all. Just a few words that I need to remember things.

The French poet Stéphane Mallarmé once talked about a dancer "writing with her body."

Naturally. But not with words. You see, I got a message. Each one of us is here to serve on this earth. And probably I was sent here to see and to hear—that's all I can do. I can't see something that doesn't exist. I don't create or invent anything, I assemble. God already made everything—colors, flowers, language—and somehow there had to be a Mother. Our business is to choose. The more you choose, the more amazing everything is. But I can't explain what I do.

How do you explain a piece by Anton Webern? You can say, mechanically, that it's twelve-tone music, but that doesn't mean anything to anybody. It's like saying something is a four-part fugue, but after a while, people listening to it lose hold of it. So the beginning of my ballet *Episodes* to Webern's music *Symphony* [Opus 21] is canonic. I had to try to paint or design time with bodies in order to create a resemblance between the dance and what was going on in sound.

The nineteenth-century theorist Eduard Hanslick said: "Music is form moving in sounds." This would also seem to be your definition of dance.

Absolutely. You have to have sound in order to dance. I need music that's possible to move to. You have to hear the music—the timbre and the use of the sound. Music is like an aquarium with the dancers inside it. It's all around you, like fish moving through water.

Some choreographers take an important piece and then give the ballet an inappropriate title—a Brahms piano concerto, say, and then call it a "Rainbow" ballet by Brahms. He didn't write a rainbow. I, personally, can't do dances to a Brahms symphony or to Beethoven—perhaps little moments from a specific piece. But you can't take one of their symphonies and dance to it.

You've choreographed much Stravinsky, but never Le Sacre du Printemps.

It's impossible, terrible. Nobody can do it. And Stravinsky's *Les Noces* is impossible, too, and it shouldn't be done. The words are tough Russian words, and when at the end of the piece the Bridegroom, very drunk, screams out that he and his Bride will live together forever and that everyone will be jealous of their good life . . . well, he's unhappy when he sings that, because the marriage will be a disaster. He's never seen her and she's never seen him. It's a tragedy, really, when you hear this sung in Russian—those words and that almost funeral music.

Speaking of Stravinsky, someone once described him at a Nadia Bou-langer class in Paris, sitting at a piano and "inventing a chord"— playing a chord, then taking one note out and putting another in until he had something very special. Don't you do the same thing?

Absolutely. There's gesture and timing, and I leave things alone or take something out, put something else in instead. I can't take a formula and do just anything with it. Naturally, in a few seconds I can create very banal movements with a formula, but to do something important, to occupy time and space with bodies—several bodies that stop in time and pass—you have to look at them and say: "Not right now, don't do that, get out, do it this way." You have to put things together like a gefilte fish. That's how I do it.

In the second pas de deux *of your ballet* Stravinsky Violin Concerto, *I get the sense of inert matter being formed—the artist shaping his materials. The dancers' last gestures, especially, suggest this. Did you have this idea in mind?*

To me, it's the music that wants you to do certain things. Dance has to look like the music. If you use music simply as an accompaniment, then you don't hear it. I occupy myself with how not to interfere with the music. And at the end of this *pas de deux* I made a gesture as if to say, "How do you do, Stravinsky?" That music is very Russian—reminiscent of old, nostalgic Russian folk songs—and I know what Stravinsky meant, I understood and felt it.

It's very difficult to make a gesture such that it looks like a sound. It's also like your asking and making a question—two people addressing the world. So, at the conclusion, I made a little bow to Stravinsky. And I also did that in the duet to the *Symphony in Three Movements*—there's a little Balinese-type gesture (Stravinsky loved Balinese culture), like a prayer, and that, too, was for the composer.

Stravinsky's body is gone, but he's still here. What could he leave, his nose? He left me a cigarette case and other things. But the music is really what he left, and when his music plays, he's right here.

There are at least two basic ideas concerning the nature of dance. The first of these is conveyed in a statement by St. Augustine: "All the dancer's gestures are signs of things, and the dance is called rational, because it aptly signifies and displays something over and above the pleasure of the senses." The second is revealed in a statement by the Sufi poet Rumi: "Whosoever knoweth the power of the dance, dwelleth in God."

To me, these are two ways of saying the same thing. Now, the dervishes don't perform specifically for the sake of money or beauty, but, personally, I have to do ballets that will attract a public. If people don't come, we don't have a company, dancers and musicians can't get paid. Once they have a salary, they can eat—and then we can tell them: "Don't eat, get thin, do this, put on some makeup, you look like hell!" *Train* them. And then you can do certain dances that aren't meant specifically to entertain the public.

In the great ballroom finale of Vienna Waltzes, *you've created a ballet that entertains but that also suggests a world of waltzing dervishes!*

I agree.

And in the midst of these whirling dancers is the heroine, who just as she seems about to awake—both sexually and spiritually—swoons and faints like the archetypal Victorian maiden.

Or like some of the characters in Turgenev . . . yes, there it is! Hegel once said that people want to see their lives onstage. That means, for example, that one man might think: "I'm married, my wife and children have left me, and I'm unhappy and feel that I'm going to kill myself. And that's what I think Art is—people should play for me my story." Another guy has a bad stomach. So everyone has a different story. Look at *Jesus Christ Superstar:* People say it's very good, they think they get something from it, but they get *nothing* from it, it's miserable. That's no way to find God—going to sleep, having a drink.

I've always wanted to know whether or not you like rock and roll.

It's not my cup of tea, I'm too old. Jazz is my time—and some Gershwin and Rodgers and Hart. But I m not really American yet. I can't under stand rock and roll words: "Auh-uh-er-er-you-er . . ." The boy and girl meet and then never meet again . . . and then . . . what . . . "you went away" . . . er . . . "you and I holding hands . . ." I don't understand it.

Getting back to dance and how you choreograph: When you first hear the opening intervals of a piece of music—Webern's Symphony—*do you immediately visualize these intervals, or feel them in your body?*

No, I feel something can be done, but if I don't try it out, then I can never do it. You can't sit down and think about dancing, you have to get up and dance. You take people and move them and see if their movements correspond to the music. And I have to know the music. In Webern's *Symphony* I made the dancers turn upside down at one point in order to parallel the use of the musical inversion. And near the ending of Stravinsky's *Movements for Piano and Orchestra* I have dancers marking the composer's returning twelve-tone row . . . but now slowed down, spread and stretched out. These certain things I do, naturally, but as little as possible. I don't imitate the notes of a piece.

When you listen to music, you can hear lots of notes in one ear, but you can't see collected movements, as if they were a pill that goes into your eye and dissolves immediately. Léonide Massine used to have people dancing everywhere—he called it contrapuntal ballet. "Contra," which means "against," actually—in reality—means "together." As I've said many times, the movements of arms, head, and feet are contrapuntal to the vertical position of the body.

Writing about Webern's use of retrograde canons, the composer Ernst Krenek once pointed to something extremely fascinating. As Krenek stated it: "The accuracy and elegance with which the reversibility of these models is worked out emanate from a peculiar fascination, seeming to suggest a mysterious possibility for circumventing the one-way direction of time." Does this have any relationship to what you feel about Webern's music or about the way you choreograph a work like Symphony?

Even if it's so, you can't and shouldn't try to effect this. Several years ago I read an article about the reverse-time sense, and I think that the world must have this sense. In the usual time sense, everything decays

—what is young gets older and separates—and the world, as we know it, is like that. But there's another world where all this decayed material, in our time sense, goes into . . . whatever it is and reverses. It's as if you're born dead, get younger, and die at birth. Not only that . . . it may be that this time sense is going on at the same time as the other one. Why not? It's everything at once. As you've reminded me before, I still believe what I once said: "I'm not interested in later on. I don't have any later on. We all live in the same time forever." . . . Of course, they talk about the Black Hole. But think: The Black Hole will probably disintegrate, too, because it's part of our world. So the Black Hole feeds himself—it's a *he*, probably, the Black Hole—he eats up the light . . . and then when he's completely fed, he'll explode like mad!

Some of the endings of your Stravinsky ballets, in particular, feel so strongly to me like beginnings that I look forward to the endings.

Like beginnings. Yes. But remember, we have to be thinking of this on the level of particles. And you don't really become aware of it, you only think of it that way. I think that the reverse-time sense is true because I've always thought that it couldn't be that everything goes in just one direction. We know Andromeda goes one way and continues to go that way until it becomes dust. But what else? What about on the level of subatomic particles? I feel something, but as Bottom the Weaver says in *A Midsummer Night's Dream*, "My eye cannot hear and my ear cannot see."

In my ballets, of course, there's an order. A dance must start and go somewhere. I can't start until I know why I have to do something. "Why this?" I say. "Why this way?" If I don't know why, I can't start a ballet. Physically, I do. But before that, I must know, I must be sure why *this* is *that* way. It's inside of me—I have to feel inside of me that this little bundle is right and that it represents something clear, with a beginning, middle, and end.

The painter Paul Klee once wrote about the idea of male sperm impregnating the egg as a way of describing the formal energy of art: "Works as form-determining sperm: the primitive male component."

I don't believe in this at all. It sounds like the painter Pavel Tchelitchew, who once described this idea in reverse. I've often said that the ballet that I represent makes the woman most important. If the woman didn't exist, there wouldn't be a ballet. It would be a man's ballet company, like Maurice Béjart's. That's a good example. There are, of course, women in his company, but it s the men—the way they look—who are most important. His *Le Sacre*, by the way, is the best anyone has done. It has a certain impact, I think, and I was amazed how almost right—physically and musically—his version was. But in my ballet, the man is a consort and the woman is the queen. Terpsichore is our muse, and little Apollo's head is covered with curls. Ballet is a feminine form, it's matriarchal. And we have to serve her.

It's strange, though—when I see your pas de deux—*especially those in* Agon, Stravinsky Violin Concerto, Duo Concertant, Pithoprakta, *I pay less attention, finally, to the fact that there's a man and a woman dancing, but rather start thinking of things like identity, personality, separation, reflections, duplications.*

That's right. Some people, though, see in these *pas de deux* only pure man-woman relationships: "The woman didn't have any guts, the man wasn't sexy enough." This isn't my business. And what you're saying is absolutely right. Strange things happen. In the Webern *(Episodes)* pas de deux, for example, it's like a roof . . . raindrops on a crystal roof.

In a pas de deux *like that I get a sense of two, or many, parts of myself, and I feel the dance as a kind of energy or electric field, lighting up my emotions.*

That's what it is. It exists.

These pas de deux *always seem to be distillations and compressions of the whole ballet, incorporating everything that occurs before and after it and raising it to an extraordinary level. "Ripeness is all," Shakespeare said. Moments of ripeness. Which reminds me of the beautiful* pas de deux *in the second act of* A Midsummer Night's Dream.

When Bottom The Weaver is transformed into an ass, he says: "The eye of man hath not heard, the ear of man hath not seen, man's hand is not able to taste, his tongue to conceive, nor his heart to report what my dream was." It sounds silly, but it's full of double and triple meanings. And I think that at moments like this, Shakespeare was a Sufi. It reminds me of St. Paul's First Epistle to the Corinthians [1 Corinthians 2:9]: "Eye hath not seen, nor ears heard, neither have entered into the heart of man, the things which God hath prepared for them that love him."

What Bottom says sounds as if the parts of the body were quarreling with each other. But it's really as if he were somewhere in the Real World. He loses his man's head and brain and experiences a revelation.

And then what happens? Bottom wants to recite his dream, which "hath no bottom," to the Duke after his and his friends' play-within-a-play is over, but the Duke chases them away. And the really deep and important message was in that dream.

At one point, when I was choreographing the ballet, I said to myself: "In the last act, I'll make a little entertainment and then a big vision of Mary standing on the sun, wrapped in the moon, with a crown of twelve stars on her head and a red dragon with seven heads and ten horns . . . the Revelation of St. John!"

Why didn't you do it?

Well, because then I thought that nobody would understand it, that people would think I was an idiot.

"The lunatic, the lover and the poet/Are of imagination all compact," Shakespeare says elsewhere in the play.

That's it. I knew it was impossible. I wished I could have done it. But instead, in the second act, I made a pretty—not silly or comic—*pas de deux* to a movement from an early Félix Mendelssohn string symphony *(Symphony No. 9 in C)*—something people could enjoy.

But that pas de deux *is so mysterious and calm . . . perhaps you did, in fact, give us Bottom's dream.*

It doesn't matter what it is. What's important is that it's pretty and makes you happy to see it. What it is—a flower or a girl or a dance or music—you can do what you want with it, you can talk about it, take it home with you, think about it, and say it represents this or that . . . that's fine.

So the inexplicability of dance is similar to Bottom's vision.

Absolutely.

You seem to choreograph these pas de deux *with a feeling of adoration and of devotion, and the result is a kind of rapturous grace.*

Naturally, I do it that way . . . but I don't tell anybody. When I was a child, I heard about a kind of enormous water lily—it was called Victoria Regina—that opens only once every hundred years. It's like wax, and everything is in there, everything lives . . . by itself, and it doesn't tell anybody anything. It goes to sleep and then comes back again. It doesn't say "Look at me, now I'm going to wake up, I'm going to jump. . . . Look, Ma, I'm dancing!" But if you happen to be around, and are ready, you'll probably see something.

It's like the time capsule with everything in it. Or like the seed that, when you plant it, becomes an enormous tree with leaves and fruit. Everything was in that little seed, and so everything can open. The tree of dance is like that. It just takes a long, long time to blossom.

[Saratoga Springs, New York, 1978]

II

Someone once suggested that painting is not a profession but actually an extension of the art of living. Do you think that might be said about dancing?

It's probably true. You see, all I am is a dancer. It started long ago, you know. At first, I didn't want to dance, but I was put in the Imperial Ballet School in Russia. I got accustomed to it and began to like it. Then I was put onstage; everyone was well-dressed in blue on a beautiful stage, and I liked participating. And it became a kind of drug. I don't know myself except as a dancer. Even now, though I'm old, I still can move, or at least I can tell exactly how it feels to move, so that I can teach and stage ballets.

You can ask a horse why he's a horse, but he just lives a horse's life. It's like the story of the horse that goes to a bar: The barman serves him, and when he leaves, the people say, "But that was a horse!" And the barman just replies, "I know, and he never takes a chaser!" So it's very difficult to explain why I do what I do. I don't live any other life. It's like a chess player who has a chess player's head.

I can teach and explain to pupils what to do better, but not because there's a reason. I got experience from wonderful teachers in Russia, and then I just started working with my body and discovered that *this* was better than *that*. I improved, I could turn, I could do everything. Now I know *why* it's this way and not that way. But that's all. People like Stravinsky and Vladimir Nabokov studied Roman law or Latin or German. They knew everything, and I didn't know anything! . . . Actually, though, I do remember that, along with my training as a dancer, I had to recite speeches by Chekhov and Aleksandr Griboyedov, and only today do I remember these. When I talk to myself now, I can recite them and appreciate that beautiful language.

You once said: "Choreography is like cooking or gardening. Not like painting, because painting stays. Dancing disintegrates. Like a garden. Lots of roses come up, and in the evening they're gone. Next day, the sun comes up. It's life. I'm connected to what is part of life."

I don't care about my past. At all. I know people like La Karinska [Barbara Karinska, former head of the NYCB costume shop], who have everything, but who only talk about the past: "I remember how I was, I was pretty, I was this and that." I don't give a damn about the past. And the future . . . I wouldn't know what that is. To me, today is everything. Of course, I remember how to cook, I remember the dough that smelled so good. *Today* comes from the past, but in reality, it's all one thing to me.

The New York City Ballet is this year [1982] celebrating the 100th anniversary of Igor Stravinsky's birth with a series of old and new ballets set to his music. You and Stravinsky were always collaborators, and it is generally agreed that there was some kind of special affinity you had with his music, and he with your choreography—as if you were soul mates.

It's difficult for me to talk about soul—I just don't know. I know, however, that I liked his music, and I felt how it should be put into movement. But our affinity with each other didn't have so much to do with soul but rather with understanding and eating food! We often had large dinners with "hookers" [Mr. Balanchine's term for a shot of vodka or whiskey] and caviar, and finally we got so that we could say dirty things, like everybody else [laughing]. But when we met to talk about his music, he'd play something and say, "This should be *this* way"—slow, fast, whatever. That's always what he did, ever since I first worked with him on *The Song of the Nightingale* in 1924 or '25.

What was your first impression of Stravinsky?

First of all, I had great respect for him; he was like my father, since he was more than twenty years older than I. Stravinsky started playing the piece on the piano—*tha ta ta ta, tha tum ta tum** . . . So I choreographed all that, and one day, Diaghilev came to see what I'd been up to and exclaimed: "No, that's the wrong tempo. Much slower!" So I changed the whole thing. Stravinsky came again, we played the piece slowly, and he said, "No, it's not right!" And I said that Mr. Diaghilev had told me to change it. Stravinsky jumped. So I rearranged the choreography again. I didn't know—I was very young, I'd never even heard the piece, I'd just come from Russia! And Matisse, whom I met . . . I didn't know who the heck Matisse was. Raphael, yes, but not Matisse! I didn't speak a word of French, but he seemed like a nice man with a beard.

Anyway, I worked with Stravinsky again on *Apollo,* and then I came to America. . . . Oh, yes, I remember meeting him in Nice, and that was easy because he spoke Russian. I had lunch at his house with his priest and the priest's wife—white clergy were allowed to marry, but not black clergy. My uncle was Archbishop of Tbilisi, by the way. And I remember that the first time he learned he was going to be a monk, he went down on the floor and was covered with black crepe. So, at that moment, he was dead to the world. Then the people helped him get up, and they took him away.

You yourself were an altar boy at church.

Yes, and I liked it. And at home, I even played priest with two chairs beside me. I liked the ceremony and the way the priests dressed. I was five or six then.

But you became a choreographer instead. Do you think there's a connection?

There is. Our church services were elaborate, like productions. They really were like plays with beautiful singing and choruses . . . You know, I've just finished choreographing Stravinsky's *Perséphone,* and at

---

* Writing in *The New York Review of Books* about this particular reminiscence (in the context of a review of the book *Portrait of Mr. B,* in which my interview was published), Stravinsky's collaborator Robert Craft states: "It should be noted . . . that Balanchine mixes memories of his first experiences of working with Stravinsky. When Balanchine sings *'tha ta ta ta, tha tum ta tum,'* he can only be indicating the first two phrases of *Apollo,* not of *Le chant du rossignol.*"

Federico Fellini on the set of Satyricon *(1969)*

Carolyn Forché

Peter Brook during his tour of Africa (1972).

Rabbi Lawrence Kushner

Marie-Louise von Franz

Dr. Oliver Sacks

Pierre Boulez

George Balanchine

Bob Dylan in his film Renaldo and Clara *(1977)*

Sam Shepard during the shooting of Country *(1984)*

the end, I bring the boys onstage—the chorus is there and nobody's doing anything—and I light them from the bottom up, so you can see their faces, as if they're candles in church.

So your childhood love of church influenced your ballets.

Oh, yes.

Stravinsky was religious. Are you?

I don't tell anyone, but I go to church by myself.

Stravinsky used to say that he believed in the Devil.

Not the Devil. The devil exists, but not the Devil. The devil only stands for the negative.

Stravinsky once wrote: "What are the connections that unite and separate music and dance? In my opinion, the one does not serve the other. There must be a harmonious accord, a synthesis of ideas. Let us speak, on the contrary, of the struggle between music and choreography."

Absolutely! Struggle means to be together. It's not so easy to unite and to be together. When you're *immediately* together, it's [clasps hands] and you evaporate. Stravinsky's right.

You see, if you look at the dances that most dance makers or ballet masters make, the music is used as background, basically . . . like movie music or television music. Who are the ballet masters? Unsuccessful dancers. Not all of them, but hundreds and hundreds everywhere. They open a school and teach badly because they didn't dance very well themselves. But to be a choreographer, you must be a great dancer—maybe not great, but better than the dancers who come to you. Because you have to invent and teach these people something that they don't know. Otherwise, you use the steps of somebody else.

I remember that with the GI Bill of Rights, the government would send us people they didn't want to take into the army, and they paid us to take them—we *had* to take them. Sixty boys would come to us. And there was one young man who approached me and asked how one became a choreographer. Well, I told him it was very difficult: You had to learn how to dance very well, better than all other dancers. And then, God blesses you, gives you something, helps you to refine what's there. And he replied: "I want to be a choreographer first. I don't want to learn anything. I want to sit and tell everybody what to do." Lots of boys were like that.

So it's no use even to talk about it. It's like everybody wants to write a book. I've even written a book, but I didn't really write it: I sat down and conversed with a nice writer, and he wrote something. So not everybody should be a choreographer. To take music and just use it as a background and have people dance to it . . . it's not right if it doesn't represent anything.

So struggle means respecting dance and music.

Yes, struggle means you have to be right in the way you put them together.

Then each of your works with Stravinsky is a struggle with his music?

Absolutely. After he finished the scores, he gave them to me. I would visit his home in California, and we'd talk. "What do you want to do?" he'd ask, and I'd say, "Supposing we do *Orpheus.*" "How do you think *Orpheus* should be done?" "Well," I'd say, "a little bit like opera. Orpheus is alone, Eurydice is dead, he cries, an angel comes and takes him to the underworld, and then Orpheus returns to earth. But he looks back, and she disappears forever."

Well, we tried to do that. And Stravinsky said, "I'll write the end first; I sometimes have an appetite to write the end first." And that's what he did, with the two horns—it's a beautiful thing, sad, hair flowing. We couldn't have a river on the stage, but it suggests something like that.

Then he asked, "Now, how to begin?" And I said, "Eurydice is in the ground, she's already buried, Orpheus is sad and cries—friends come to visit him, and then he sings and plays." "Well," Stravinsky asked, "how long does he play?" And I started to count [snaps fingers], the curtain goes up. "How long would you like him to stand without dancing, without moving? A sad person stands for a while, you know." "Well," I said, "maybe at least a minute." So he wrote down "minute." "And then," I said, "his friends come in and bring something and leave." "How long?" asked Stravinsky. I calculated it by walking. "That will take about two minutes." He wrote it down.

And it went on like that. He'd say, "I want to know how long it should be." "It could be a little longer," I'd tell him, "but at least it's not forever!" And later he played one section for me, and I said, "It's a little bit too short." "Oh, oh," he'd sigh, "I already orchestrated it, and it's all finished. . . . Well, I'll do something, I know what to do." "Ah, thank you!" I replied. Things like that, you see: "How long?" he'd say. "One minute and twenty seconds," I'd tell him. "Twenty-*one,*" he'd say, and smile. And I'd agree, "Fine, twenty-one!"

Stravinsky is more complicated than I am, because the body doesn't have the possibilities that music has in terms of speed. A pianist can play fast, but the body can't go that quickly. The body's different from music. Supposing you start moving fast, like sixty-fourth notes. But you can't, you can't see it. Eyes can't really see peripherally, the movement passes and is gone. So we have to calculate movements. To hear and to see isn't the same thing. You have to have extremely fantastic eyes to see everything.

But perhaps it's better not to talk about. Horses don't talk, they just go! We want to win the race. And how? With energy, training, and dancing!

[New York City, 1982]

Pierre Boulez

"I BELIEVE A CIVILIZATION THAT CONSERVES," THE FRENCH COM-
poser and conductor Pierre Boulez once stated, "is one that will decay
because it is afraid of going forward and attributes more importance to
memory than the future. The strongest civilizations are those without
memory—those capable of complete forgetfulness. They are strong
enough to destroy because they know they can replace what is destroyed. Today our musical civilization is not strong: it shows clear signs
of withering."

Along with Karlheinz Stockhausen and Luciano Berio, Pierre Boulez
(who was born in 1925 in Montbrison, France) is probably the most
important European composer since World War II—the creator of such
extraordinary works as *Le Marteau Sans Maître*, *Pli Selon Pli*, *Éclat-Multi-
ples*, *Rituel*, and *Notations for Orchestra*. He has always been an audacious,
recusant, and outspoken avant-garde polemicist, who once, as a student
—accompanied by ten like-minded noisy compatriots—invaded a Stravinsky concert to protest that composer's "reactionary neoclassicism."
An early and ardent advocate of "serialism" (a procedure in which
musical parameters such as pitch, dynamics, and rhythm are predeter-
mined by the composer), Boulez dismissed Arnold Schoenberg—the
founder of the "Twelve-Tone School"—as a failed revolutionary in an
infamous 1951 article entitled "Schoenberg Is Dead." And he more
than once rhetorically suggested that it would be no loss if the opera
houses of the world were blown up.

All this from a man who would eventually conduct astonishing and
illuminating performances of Wagner's *Ring* cycle at Bayreuth, *Pelléas
and Mélisande* at Covent Garden, and *Wozzeck* and *Lulu* at the Paris
Opera. But Boulez has also stated: "I am not much given to settling
down in positions that have already been won. You must always keep
questioning yourself." And he has done so, both in his recent, partly
electronic compositions such as . . . *explosante/fixe* . . . and *Répons*
and as a conductor of the music of Debussy, Ravel, Stravinsky, Schoen-

here, Alban Berg, Webern, Charles Ives, and Edgard Varèse. In fact, with his profound sense of rhythmic precision, timbral clarity, and structural definition, Boulez, as chief conductor of the BBC Symphony Orchestra and musical director and chief conductor of the New York Philharmonic, gradually revealed himself as our preeminent interpreter of twentieth-century music. As the first and current director of IRCAM *(Institut de Recherche et de Coordination Acoustique/Musique)*—the subterranean musical research center of Centre Georges Pompidou—moreover, Boulez has single-handedly put Paris at the forefront of contemporary musical life, a position it has not occupied since the Middle Ages and the first part of our century. As a composer, conductor, writer, teacher, and administrator, Boulez is "beyond question"—in the opinion of the English music critic Peter Heyworth—"one of the dominant musical figures of our time."

Concerning his notion of what he considers most valuable in musical creation, Boulez once said: "I like a work to be a labyrinth—one should be able to lose oneself in it. A work whose course reveals itself completely at one hearing is flat and lacking in mystery. The mystery of a work resides precisely in its being valid at many different levels. Whether it be a book, a picture, or a piece of music, these polyvalent levels of interpretation are fundamental to my conception of the work." In today's musically fractious world, however—whose fruitful diversity happily compensates for its state of divisiveness—not every composer would concur with Boulez's musical credo. Yet it is, I believe, one worth heeding and admiring—both for its preceptual rigor and for the musical richnesses and resonances it allows, and even argues for, under its seemingly detached, formal, and protective aesthetic shield.

I interviewed an extremely busy but gracious Pierre Boulez—who speaks a characteristically rapid, precise, and lucid English—in his underground office at IRCAM in April 1984. The subject of our discussion: the state of contemporary music.

*   *   *

The state of contemporary music seems to me to be unusually similar to that of contemporary architecture. As the critic Ada Louise Huxtable, writing in The New York Review of Books, *recently stated: "There is no* Zeitgeist *demanding recognition and fealty, no unifying force or sentiment, no greater public good, no banner around which architects can rally. They can go in any direction and follow any muse. This is surely one of the most open, challenging, promising, and dangerous moments in the history of the building art." Don't you think that this is true of the composing art as well?*

Yes and no. When I hear about the "Return to Romanticism," for example, I recall that the real romantics of the nineteenth century were extremely adventurous. But what I see in many of today's musical currents is simply a dead solution—a kind of self-protection against what is going on right now. There are, on the contrary, some other directions which seem to me more alive—the creation of new material and new aspects of sound, for instance. There are still some composers who recognize the adventure and who aren't afraid of going somewhere without knowing exactly where they will finish. And to me this is very important. The previous generation of composers was very adventurous, but that of the neoclassical 1930s, say, reflected the end of invention. And I think that right now we are witnessing the same kind of protective phenomenon. Ada Louise Huxtable mentioned the word *Zeitgeist,* but I would use the word *Angst* in this case. Because there is a kind of anxiety in trying to find a refuge in old values that are no longer relevant.

The American composer Jacob Druckman recently [1983] programmed a series of contemporary music concerts for the New York Philharmonic subtitled, "Since 1968 a New Romanticism?" (There was a question mark in there.)

The question mark was very important, too!

And Druckman classified music as being either Apollonian—logical, rational, chaste—or Dionysian—sensual, mysterious, ecstatic. But if one thinks of a composition such as your own Livre Pour Cordes—*just to take one of numerous examples—it's obvious how simplistic and artificial Druckman's classification really is.*

This distinction between Dionysian and Apollonian is one that was made long ago by Nietzsche, and it had a meaning at that time. But these terms, which are very important, are now devalued to the point where they just become simple market words. For me, the deep problem of music is not whether it is either rational or ecstatic, but whether and how it allows you to express yourself. And if you're a complicated self, you express yourself in more complicated terms. In poetry, Mallarmé was expressing himself in a much more difficult way than [Paul]

Verlaine—all human minds aren't built on the same model. The opposition, then, is really between that of being understood or not being understood by the mass, between being complex or not complex, between having a vocabulary which is really very easy or one that is less easy to grasp. That's much more the problem; and hiding behind false categories is, to me, simply that.

Frank Zappa, who performs rock and roll for the masses, recently completed an orchestral score entitled **The Perfect Stranger** *that you conducted in Paris. [Boulez has since recorded this score with the Ensemble Inter Contemporain for Angel/EMI records.]*

Yes, he didn't want to be imprisoned in jail, in his musical ghetto. I think this kind of exchange is important. Because in the "classical" realm, we, too, are in a kind of ghetto and suffer under the weight of all these traditions, with their constraints of spirit and ways of thinking. I think it's very good to be in touch with people who have other concepts, and maybe they'll be freed of *their* concepts by meeting us, and vice versa.

You once stated: "Nothing could be more fruitful than this perpetual modification of perspective, of hypotheses, in the face of musical reality. . . . I am not much given to settling down in positions that have already been won. You must always keep questioning yourself." So your view of music is basically a dialectical one.

Completely. But I don't give up my principles, since to me that's just laziness.

So you wouldn't follow, say, George Rochberg's lead in giving up "twelve-tone" music and composing like Gustav Mahler instead.

Definitely not. Because I think Mahler has done it much better than Mr. Rochberg will ever do.

Sometimes I think that a dyed-in-the-wool conservative composer like Samuel Barber wrote better "romantic" music than most of today's so-called neoromanticists.

Yes, because for him that was genuine—that was his way of thinking, his way of expressing himself. All right, his music wasn't terribly advanced, but at least it was honest. And what I fear in this type of "neoromanticism" is its deep dishonesty—dishonesty with oneself and with the audience—and, ultimately, an avoidance of real musical problems.

It is a commonplace that the modernist architectural movement of the first part of the century valued the notions of "function," "purification," and "salvation through design"; distrusted historical allusion and ornament; and emphasized planes, solids, and voids, thereby eliminating reference to the outside world. Similarly, in early twentieth-century music we find the case of Anton Webern, whose works you once called the "threshold of the music of the future," practicing and preaching an aesthetic that focused on "natural musical laws"; on symmetries, analogies, and groupings; and on "the unity and utmost relatedness of all component parts." But nowadays you find an architect like Robert Venturi praising "elements which are hybrid rather than pure, compromising rather than clean, distorted rather than straightforward, ambiguous and equivocal rather than direct and clear. I am for messy vitality," Venturi states, "over obvious unity." And many of today's composers would certainly agree with these sentiments.

But I don't necessarily disagree with Venturi's point of view. Because, as a matter of fact, the excess of purity always brings an excess of impurity. You can see that very well throughout the history of architecture. Baroque architecture was very impure in this sense—and also very interesting—but this doesn't mean that Baroque architecture should simply be opposed to Romanesque architecture just because the latter is very simple and the former is overcharged. No, I find it a bit childish to put things in this black-and-white manner.

Of course, with Webern you had an excess of purity, but it was necessary in his case—maybe because of his personality, first of all—but also because the birth of the new language was very difficult, and it couldn't accept ornamentation at that moment. But to prolong this ascetic attitude out of context would be unnatural today, since now you need something that is more ornate, richer in texture, more contrasted—a kind of enrichment of this language. But it doesn't mean that because you wish to enrich the thinking of your predecessors, you therefore have to go back to their predecessors—that because you don't want the Mies van der Rohe approach you have to return to the nineteenth century. It seems really stupid to me that in order to avoid a present danger, you adopt the dangers of the previous generation. In this way, you don't go forward and rethink a situation. And it doesn't work. This was like Stravinsky in the twenties saying: "I want to be 'classical,' so I will imitate the style of Bach." That was a completely useless reaction. And I can already see now that our "new" postmodernist buildings are as dead . . . even deader than the ones they wanted to replace.

As Ada Louise Huxtable has asked: "How many false columns and gables, how many cut-out oculi *and post-Palladian screens, how many deco touches and diagonal plans, how much ad hoc jumble does it take to add up to a predictable postmodernist cliché?"*

Exactly. I call that the aesthetical supermarket. You can have fruits from China, vegetables from Brazil, and think you're having a really good meal. But it's nothing to do with art.

That doesn't sound like such a bad meal to me!

It all depends on what you mix!

What about the important and often fruitful influence of Asiatic and early Western musical ideas, techniques, and textures on works as different as, say, Steve Reich's Tehillim *and your own* Éclat—*not to forget the obvious and earlier example of Debussy?*

Definitely, but you're always influenced by something; and when you discover a new culture you're going to be affected by it. But it's one thing to grasp the exterior part and quite another to understand the spirit of that influence. Even Debussy spoke of Japanese theater as if there were nothing complicated about it—he thought you just needed a couple of noises and voices shouting somewhere and you could then create the greatest tragedy in the world! But he didn't realize that Japanese theater was absolutely ritualistic and governed by more laws than anything we have in the West.

A great deal of misunderstanding occurs when you approach another civilization because, looking at it from outside, you miss or misspell the laws. But I find that these misunderstandings are often very fruitful, since what you see in another culture is what you want that other culture to reveal about what you *yourself* are doing and searching for. And then suddenly, you find something in common and you take from this culture what you most need. When you're creative, you look at everything in life as a predator. Even the most trivial things can strike you as exactly the thing you were waiting for just at that moment. Newton's apple, for example, didn't make him think of his computations. But he was thinking of them, and then this trivial occurrence led him in the right direction. And I think that we all are waiting for Newton's apple to fall on our heads!

Debussy once wrote: "Discipline must be sought in freedom and not within the formulas of an outworn philosophy." And many people have criticized the so-called "serial" compositions of the fifties and sixties for not heeding Debussy's advice and trying rather to find freedom in discipline.

I think that's too simple a distinction. Because the procedures of a composer are very closely related to the period in which he's living. Now, although Debussy's vocabulary was new, the elements—the perfect triads, etc.—were not. Debussy was free with regard to the network of musical relationships, but he was not with regard to the construction of the objects themselves. So for him the problem was simply to free the objects of the kind of constraints they'd previously been bound by.

Now, in our time, especially in the fifties, you had a new vocabulary and you didn't want any familiar musical objects to be there, so you had to construct them. And then you understood that you couldn't build objects without laws. Debussy built his chords based on "known" laws —they were used constantly, so he didn't have to think about them. But in the fifties you had to think about the methods of building these objects, so therefore the situation wasn't at all the same. Debussy's world was coherent, and he brought fantasy to it; while our world was incoherent, and we had to bring coherence to it . . . but without losing fantasy. And this was a problem that wasn't easy to solve. Because if you were too much engulfed in the methodology, then you lost complete spontaneity. The great composers throughout history have always tried to find a balance between spontaneity and strength of ideas. The stronger they were and the kinds of constraints they created for themselves enabled them to bring their imaginations into a world they would never have reached otherwise.

Philip Glass once stated that the compositions written in the fifties by you, Stockhausen, and Henri Pousseur, among others, seemed "creepy" both to him and to many of his generation.

Yes, but fights between generations are natural because you have always to find yourself, your own personality. It happens in families, it happens in life generally, so why not in the arts?

But polemics aside—which may be amusing but not finally terribly interesting—I think simply that suddenly there was a reaction against what was the "action" before. I wonder what it will be like in twenty years. Because in 1944 and 1945, for example, all the people of the Paris school—Francis Poulenc, Georges Auric, and so on—were saying that Schoenberg was out of fashion and old hat. And they were writing music of the third category—entertainment music, light music—and it had an audience. But as a matter of fact, what remains in history—entertainment music or music that is more demanding and interesting because it brings out more of the human experience? If you want a kind of supermarket aesthetic, okay, do that, nobody will be against it, but everybody will eventually forget it because each generation will create its own supermarket music—like produce that after eight days is rotten and you can't eat it anymore and have to toss it away. And, therefore, I'm always astonished that composers speak in terms of quantity, i.e., "Music is valid if it has more than two thousand people listening to it." For me, that's no criterion of validity. And when composers say that they've found a direct approach to an audience, what is that really? The "direct approach" is usually an experience that the audience has already had but with a new coat of paint on it, so to speak—that's all. And that's not a new experience. I find that very superficial and an avoidance of the real problems and symptomatic of a kind of amnesia that has forgotten about the catastrophes of previous years—the "stereophonic" year, the "chance" year, the "formless" year, the "novel tone colors" year. Even the works of a movement like neoclassicism are hardly performed anymore. So I'm afraid that some of the composers who are the excitement of today will not be the excitement of tomorrow; their works are, as they say in German, *Plakate*—advertising posters.

To be more specific, you have said that today's popular minimalist/ repetitive composers make pieces in which the musical material "moves without moving." But, in fact, many of these compositions have an immediate and moving effect on its audience.

I don't want to be derogatory, but I think that that type of music appeals to an extremely primitive perception, and it reduces the elements of music to one single component—periodicity. You have a chord changing slowly, and the rest of the components are either completely ignored or reduced to just a minimum of minimums. And people suddenly say, "Ah, my god! I understand modern music!" But it's not modern whatsoever. It's simply like a detail of a painting that's been enlarged many times, and there's no substance to it whatsoever. If an audience wants to get high with this kind of music rather than with another product, that's okay with me. But I don't consider that a very high level of enjoyment.

Now, you can be obsessive in music without being simplistic. In Stravinsky, for instance, you have a lot of repetitive patterns—I'm thinking particularly of *Les Noces*—but they are manipulated in much more interesting ways. The music is rather reduced in its components, but it has a dialectic and a kind of evolution that makes things live. On the contrary, when you've heard two minutes of one of these recent minimal works, you know very well where it goes. And I find that, for me, if there's no surprise, then I'm no longer interested in it. Similarly, when you see light sculptures based on periodicity and are told that you won't have a similar periodicity for another two hundred years, well, who's interested in looking at that? That's just being passive. To me it's like cows in front of a train. And there are people who listen to music in this way.

It's frequently been said about totally serialized compositions, though, that if every musical event is different, then everything becomes and sounds the same.

I dealt with this problem myself, long ago—in 1955, in fact. And certainly, if you're constantly varying the parameters of composition, nobody can distinguish anything. The French philosopher Gilles Deleuze has said that perception is based on repetition and difference. And that's why I think it's necessary to have a certain form of repetition, because perception requires articulation fields to let you know where you are. And you can know where you are only when you can recognize similarities. But some things should only *seem* similar, because if they're too much alike then they'll repeat themselves, and the fourth time will be exactly the same as the third, and the third like the second. And if you can foresee this, the work is dead. Immediately. Because as soon as you can predict the combinations, it's superfluous for the composer to proceed with them. So why do it? For me what's interesting is to present material that is evolving and then, from time to time, to bring back the model . . . but not in exactly the same way. So that a listener has to wonder, "Do I recognize it? Don't I recognize it? I'm not sure anymore But I know that it has something to do with it." And in *this* sense I like ambiguity—to get back to Robert Venturi's comment. But the kind of ambiguity that's simply a matter of games and style doesn't interest me at all.

This, for me, is the difference between, for instance, the late Picasso and, say, Jackson Pollack. You look at one of Picasso's later paintings for two minutes, and you know very well how it's been done, you've understood everything. But if you observe the best works of Pollack, you're puzzled and you try to see and explore his labyrinth; and that makes the work interesting and sustains your attention. Of course, you can be lost at first, but after a kind of acquaintance with the painting, you've lived with it and it changes. But the simplistic works, in their relationships with you, don't change. And that's their death.

Another example in this respect is Kafka, because he also constructs a kind of labyrinth where the logic is perfect, but it leads you into areas that are completely unexpected, such that you think you're going one way and then you wind up in the other direction. And I've found that when you're composing a work, it's exactly the same—you don't want to know at the onset where you'll be at the end of the score. You have a vague idea, of course, but it's not a matter of going in a straight line, you have all kinds of divigations.

You've spoken about the legendary Chinese landscape painter who disappeared into his canvas. And in many of your works, you seem to create moments of almost Oriental transparency and particularity that are then counterbalanced by moments of chaos—suggesting a movement from hyperconsciousness to the realm of the unconscious.

I myself like this kind of approach, so it's reflected in what I'm doing. And since this is what I like in painting and literature, I also want to express it in music, because it's certainly my personality—to be crystal clear in the sense that sometimes the crystal reflects yourself and other times you can see through the material. So the work suggests a hiding and opening at the same time. And what I want most to create is a kind of deceiving transparency, as if you are looking in very transparent water and can't make an estimation of the depths.

And when you stir things up . . .

That's when you begin to know.

Schoenberg once asserted: "Either what we do is music or what the French do is music. But both cannot be music." If one takes a wider view of the history of modern music, however, it seems clear that a lot of the sectarianism and partisanship reflected in Schoenberg's remark overlooks some important similarities between seemingly "antithetical" compositions such as Schoenberg's Farben *and Olivier Messiaen's* Chronochromie, *Debussy's* Les Parfums de la Nuit *and Berg's* Three Pieces for Orchestra, *Varèse's* Ionization *and Elliott Carter's* Double Concerto, *and even certain works by Webern and Morton Feldman.*

I find that composers tend to concentrate their attention on very specific aspects of music. But, of course, if they're very gifted, they can't neglect the other aspects; and even if these aspects aren't consciously always on their minds, composers still work unconsciously with them. We can say that a composer has a very solid center and then a kind of diffuse surrounding, and he's responsible for the center but less directly responsible for the rest. That's the influence of the outside world and of other composers. Even if they have their own territory really well guarded, all composers have buffer zones. And some of the musical aspects of these zones do relate in surprising ways to the works of other composers, such that there are similarities that even the composers themselves might be surprised by.

I've even felt a connection between the rhythmic aspects of the music of Schoenberg and Paul Hindemith, though it would undoubtedly have surprised and shocked both of them to hear that said.

Definitely. *Moses and Aaron* is Hindemith's greatest opera—an opera that Hindemith might have dreamt of writing but was never able to do . . . I'm sure of that. But don't forget the period of the thirties was neoclassicist, and neoclassicism's vocabulary implied certain kinds of rhythmical patterns, distribution of voices, and so on. And, in this case, Schoenberg was more refined and more effective than Hindemith, since the latter worked on a more primitive level. But I'm sure that Schoenberg wrote the best works of Hindemith!

Referring to the music of Charles Ives, John Cage once asked: "Does it emerge? Or do we enter in?" And Cage suggested that the former was most often the case, stating: "The difference is this: Everybody hears the same thing if it emerges. Everybody hears what he alone hears if he enters in." But if one thinks of supposedly "emerging" compositions like

Elliott Carter's string quartets on your own Pli Selon Pli, *it's obvious that each listener will hear and discover quite different things in such richly layered works.*

Proust once said—and of course he phrased it more brilliantly than I can—that when you read a book, you're discovering yourself, and what you discover there is what you need. The only thing that a writer can be glad of, Proust added, is that his work can help somebody else to live his own life. And I agree with this completely.

[Paris, 1984]

Carolyn Forché

WHEN IT COMES TO POETRY, IT IS ALWAYS THE BEST OF TIMES AND the worst of times. The bad news is that, generally speaking, books of poetry sell fewer than four thousand copies; and our larger publishing houses are increasingly less interested in putting out collections of verse. "Poetry publishing has always been an endangered species, even before economic pressures sent publishers in search of mass audiences for their books," Barney Rosset of Grove Press stated in 1982 in announcing a welcome new poetry series. And he added: "Now the threat of extinction is greater than ever. But we cannot hope for vigorous literature tomorrow unless we keep alive an audience—no matter what size—for the new poets of today."

The good news is that, although unknown to many people, there are scores of marvelous poets who are writing and publishing in this country. On just one of my poetry bookshelves, for example, I can easily point to several excellent works of the past few years: James Schuyler's *The Morning of the Poem*, Diane di Prima's *Loba*, Antler's *Factory*, Anne Waldman's *First Baby Poems*, and the late Kenneth Rexroth's *The Morning Star*. Right next to these are also a few of the many magnificent recent volumes of translations: Robert Bly's versions of Tomas Tranströmer, Guy Davenport's Archilochus, Stephen Mitchell's Rilke, Howard Norman's *The Wishing Bone Cycle* (poems from the Swampy Cree Indians), Randy Blasing and Mutlu Konuk's renditions of the great Turkish poet Nazim Hikmet, Jonathan Chaves's readings of the Ming Dynasty Chinese poet Yüan Hung-tao, and poet/editor Paul Auster's path-breaking *The Random House Book of Twentieth-Century French Verse*. And finally, there are indispensable volumes—some published posthumously—of collected and selected poems by exemplary writers such as George Oppen, William Bronk, Galway Kinnell, James Merrill, David Ignatow, William Stafford, Louis Zukofsky, Muriel Rukeyser, Elizabeth Bishop, Charles Reznikoff, and Lorine Niedecker.

In fact, there are as many, and as many kinds of, significant poets publishing today as there are readers with their particular aesthetic and formal preferences and social concerns. To mention the names of poets such as June Jordan, John Ashbery, Leslie Scalapino, Ai, Miguel Algarin, Adrienne Rich, Charles Simic, Ray Young Bear, Amy Clampitt, Robert Duncan, Jack Gilbert, Amiri Baraka, Mary Oliver, Michael Palmer, Robert Kelly, Gary Snyder, and Clarence Major is only to give a hint of the diversity of present-day American poetry. And while the large publishing houses are withdrawing their commitment to contemporary poetry (university presses, of course, are a valuable mainstay), one should note that a number of important smaller presses—e.g., North Point Press, Black Sparrow, Grey Wolf, Copper Canyon Press, Sun & Moon Books, Station Hill, Sun, and Momo's Press—are taking on and filling an increasingly necessary and vital cultural role.

*   *   *

Perhaps no one better exemplifies the power and excellence of contemporary poetry then Carolyn Forché, who is not only one of the most affecting younger poets in America but also one of the best poets writing anywhere in the world today. Born in Detroit in 1950, Forché won the Yale Series of Younger Poets Award in 1976 for her first book, *Gathering the Tribes*—a dazzling collection of poems about her indomitable Slavic grandmother, Anna; her working-class childhood and childhood sweetheart, Joey; her visits with and descriptions of the Indian and Spanish poor in the American Southwest; her bittersweet romantic relationships; and her mysterious, passionate, almost mythical encounter with a woman stranger on a beach in the Pacific Northwest ("Kalaloch").

Her second book, *The Country Between Us* (Harper & Row, 1981), was chosen as the Lamont Selection of the Academy of American Poets, and has elicited enormous praise from writers such as Denise Levertov, Margaret Atwood, and Jacobo Timerman. (In its first year of publication, it sold about twenty thousand copies, making it that rarest of things—a poetry best-seller.) The collection contains a number of dark, lyrical remembrances and evocations of childhood friends, lovers, strangers, and, again, the writer's grandmother—each of these meditations revealing a remarkable verbal power and mastery of imagery, an amazing ability to move swiftly from one realm of feeling and consciousness to another, and a tone of voice that suggests, in the words of poet Miguel Hernandez, "the joyful sadness of the olive tree."

But *The Country Between Us* has undoubtedly gained its unusually large readership because of its opening section—a series of eight overwhelming, harrowing poems about El Salvador, where Forché spent two years on and off, as a human-rights investigator, political journalist, and sympathizer of the victims of what Walt Whitman once called the "real war" that "never gets in the books." In her poems, Forché is a witness not only to the cruelties of the Salvadoran (and, more generally, the Central American) civil war, but to the lack of attention, compassion, and commitment of those of us who, as she writes in "Return," were "born to an island of greed/and grace where you have this sense/ of yourself as apart from others." As she concludes in "Ourselves or Nothing," the final poem of her book:

> In the mass graves, a woman's hand
> caged in the ribs of her child,
> a single stone in Spain beneath olives,
> in Germany the silent windy fields,
> in the Soviet Union where the snow
> is scarred with wire, in Salvador
> where the blood will never soak
> into the ground, everywhere and always
> go after that which is lost.
> There is a cyclone fence between
> ourselves and the slaughter and behind it
> we hover in a calm protected world like
> netted fish, exactly like netted fish.
> It is either the beginning of the end
> of the world, and the choice is ourselves
> or nothing.

The following conversation took place in New York City in October of 1982 during one of Carolyn Forché's poetry reading tours. (She is, incidentally, a brilliant and illuminating reader of her verse.) She is currently living part of the year abroad, the other part working with her photographer-husband Harry Mattison on a documentary book about unemployed mine workers in the Iron Range of northern Minnesota.

* * *

Walt Whitman once wrote: "The proof of a poet is that his country absorbs him as affectionately as he has absorbed it." How do you see the state of American poetry today?

I was talking to a poet the other day and he said something very interesting: "I feel," he told me, "that I'm in exile in my own country." And it seems to me that much of the poetry written today is about this exile. In a way, there's a tendency for poets to abandon the culture at large and to write about the alienation that they feel. Throughout the seventies, I noticed a poetry of refined and elegant language, which somehow seemed to convey this sense of being detached from the culture. Many young poets who grew up in small towns were writing poetry that read as if they'd spent their childhoods in Europe, had the benefit of a classical education, and had the luxury to develop a kind of distanced boredom. You get the impression that they lived very differently from the way they really did. There were exceptions, of course; but a lot of the poetry during the past decade seemed more descriptive of itself than it was about any kind of reality outside. Poets were pretty much writing for each other. And so they probably shouldn't complain today about the narrowness of their audiences because it hasn't particularly been their concern to address a large number of readers and listeners. But, of course, we've also seen a more general kind of diminishment and extreme introspection in our American culture during the past ten years— a departure from music, from art, from poetry, from political action.

What do you think of the writing programs in universities today?

They've become too institutionalized, a bit too much of a club, and I think that most of the writers involved with writing programs would agree that this is the case. It's dangerous when a writing program presumes to do something that it just can't do. I mean, it does not *make* the writer, all it can do is give him or her an opportunity to write and maybe teach writing, if that's something a person wants to do, for a couple of years. For me, it was an opportunity to live in a community with other young writers.

I would hope that many writers would choose *not* to train themselves in that way, however. I favor apprenticing oneself to a mentor, a writer whom one regards very highly, developing a relationship with that author's work and perhaps eventually with him or her as a teacher. I've had very good experiences as a workshop teacher, and I've had very ugly ones as well where . . . I don't know what to say the workshop was about, but it wasn't necessarily about poetry. And there's a tendency for a certain kind of poem to emerge that is considered "acceptable," and that can be dangerous.

Yet, in another way, I want the programs to exist because they're very good for many writers at certain points in their lives; I just wish that they weren't regarded in quite the way they've been in the last decade. You see, I didn't have any money when I went to school, and when I left the university I had to pay off an enormous debt for my tuition. I would have had to have worked a nine-to-five job, and it's very difficult to write if you come home exhausted. So working through a Master of Fine Arts program gave me the opportunity to write my first book, which then afforded me the opportunity to teach, which gave me a schedule enabling me to write. The schedule when I first taught at San Diego State University was very grueling, but, just the same, there's no comparison between that kind of work and forty hours a week punching a clock. It helped me, and therefore I can't disparage writing programs because there will be many writers in the position I was in as well; and I would hate to see the work in this culture be produced only by those who can afford to produce it. It's a bit of snobbery just to say, "Aren't writing programs awful!" I'm suspicious of that attitude as well.

When did you first start writing poetry?

I was about nine years old—the oldest of seven children living in Farmington, Michigan. My father was at work, we were all home from school because there was a blizzard outside, and my mother said, "Why don't you write a poem?" And she took out and dusted off her college poetry textbook—she had gone to college for two years before she married—and she showed me what a poem was. She explained to me what a metrical foot was, and she made the little markings and taught me the stresses. She read me some poems, and she laid them all out. And I looked at these things, and right away I went and wrote a poem which, very unimaginatively, was about snow. I began to work in iambic pentameter because I didn't know there was anything else, but I was absolutely taken with writing verse.

I think I used writing as an escape. Writing and daydreaming. Writing was simply the reverie that I recorded, and I wrote volumes of diaries and journals. And then when I wasn't writing, when I was doing housework or whatever, I kept some sort of little voice running in my mind. I told myself narratives, and I made a parallel life to my own. It was completely imaginary, and most of the time everything would take place a hundred years earlier . . . on the same spot where I was. I suspected, when I was young, that this was madness, but I couldn't give it up. Then I lost the voice, the capacity to do this for hours and hours—I lost it when I was about seventeen. And it was horrifying to realize that it was gone. For me it was the end of my childhood. And my mind changed. But as I developed, I wrote more consciously.

So poetry began with my mother. She talked to me a lot when I was very young, but as the years went by, she didn't have any time. Yet what she gave me when I was nine was one of those rare, beautiful moments. And that moment was enough to last for a long time.

Your first volume of poems, Gathering the Tribes, *is an amazingly assured work. When did you find your own voice?*

I was twenty-four when I completed that book. It was selected by the Yale Series of Younger Poets when I was twenty-five and published when I was twenty-six. It represents work from age nineteen to age twenty-four, but from age nine to age nineteen I wrote terribly.

When I was thirteen I discovered free verse by reading e.e. cummings, but I didn't understand free verse at all. I thought, "Well, it's scattered all over the page, you don't need to do it metrically, you can just use these little phrases and scatter them around . . . and you can do *whatever you want.*" So I started writing nonsense, just nonsense; and I was writing in lowercase *i*'s all over, and it was just awful. I wrote my best work during that period in Catholic school, which I attended for twelve years. The nuns used to assign us to write paragraphs, and these were wonderful little passages of description, but my poetry was awful. I'm interested in prose, too; I don't make this division between poetry and prose too much because I think of poetry in a broader sense.

I work very slowly. I have to revise and discard a great deal because I write things that aren't worth sharing or troubling other people with, really. And then it was hard to write after the first book was published. All of a sudden I couldn't do it. I was very shy when I was young—I was used to being on the periphery of things, just watching. And after my book was published, I would walk into a room and was suddenly no longer a person on the periphery, but the author of this particular book. It was very difficult for me—I made a lot of errors in judgment, emotional errors, I didn't know how to be someone who was spoken to or focused upon in that way. I didn't like anything that I wrote, and finally I *couldn't* write. I became ill with spinal meningitis in 1976. And when I got well I wrote another poem, almost inadvertantly, before I remembered that I wasn't able to do so anymore [laughing], and that was "For the Stranger," which is the oldest work in the second book. It came all of a piece, all at once. And there was something odd about it, the voice had changed.

The voice in my first book doesn't know what it thinks, it doesn't make any judgments. All it can do is perceive and describe and use language to make some sort of re-creation of moments in time. But I noticed that the person in the second book makes an utterance. And in a way it was a little haunting to realize that some sort of maturation had occurred unconsciously.

In your early poem "Burning the Tomato Worms," you quote your Slavic grandmother, Anna, as saying: "Mother of God/I can tell you this/Dushenka/You work your life/You have nothing." And it strikes me that a lot of women you write about—the impoverished Spanish and Indian women in the American Southwest, the peasant women in El Salvador—could say this as well. And there's a sense of comradeship you seem to feel with these and other women in your poetry.

The strongest influences in my life have been women—my grandmother, my mother, many older women. With one exception, every one who taught me in El Salvador was female—*compañeras*—which means something more than "companion."

The reality is that women are oppressed and becoming more impoverished by the year, even in *this* country. Single women with their dependent children are forming a new, economically depressed underclass, and women of all classes and races are affected by an erosion of the previous decade's gains. Women of certain position and education have made great strides, but those strides, to my way of thinking, have all been at the top. In other words, we might have women pilots and women vice presidents of corporations, but the lot of most women has deteriorated. I've read that more than eighty percent of fathers of families, after one year of divorce, cease to contribute to child support.

I feel most compelled by women; I'm more deeply affected by them —maybe because I was raised by my mother and grandmother, and then educated by nuns—I suppose it couldn't help but happen. And I think that oppression has in many women fostered a kind of strength that is incomparable.

Your grandmother, Anna, seems like an incomparably strong woman.

When I first traveled to Eastern Europe, Anna was everywhere. I felt as if she had come back to me, and I felt her *in* me, too. I had her with me until I was eighteen and then she died. And it wasn't enough time, really—I didn't get to ask her the most important questions. And now I have to live those questions myself. I know the kind of life she had when she came to this country, working in the needle factory and her husband in the coke ovens. I don't have illusions about her—she was a strong and domineering woman. She was a peasant woman, and so when I went to El Salvador and spent time with the *campesinos*, I didn't feel as uncomfortable or self-conscious as I might have without having had Anna as my grandmother.

Your epigram to the first section of your second book, The Country Between Us, *is by the Spanish poet Antonio Machado, and it says: "Walker, there is no road/You make your own way as you walk." Your own poems, of course, mirror your own path—one that has taken you on all kinds of open roads. You seem to be a voracious traveler.*

If I indulge myself, I could say that there's been a sort of ongoing pattern or mysterious and compelling force in my life. But when I think about the reasons for my traveling, I could also say that my grandmother Anna was a wanderer, and that my aunt once told me that in every generation in my family there's been a woman who hasn't been able to settle in one place. And they all thought that I was the one; they decided that "Carolyn goes off because she's Anna, she's got that restlessness in her." Also, when I traveled to the American Southwest, I was getting over the death of a friend, and I went there to wander around and was taken in by an older Indian couple in a pueblo in northern New Mexico. They gave me meals, and gradually I was taught a little Tewa, and one thing led to another. Always, wherever I would go, this seemed to happen.

I had very difficult, sad times in my early adulthood, and I thought, "Well, I'm not responsible for what has happened to me, but I *am* responsible for my responses. So I have to respond well or else become deranged." Then, midway through my twenties, it occurred to me that I was also responsible for what happened to me, that I had a certain amount of choice, and that the ways in which I tended could determine events. So when I first felt the urge to translate the Salvadoran poet Claribel Alegría,* who lives in exile in Mallorca, I realized that I was ignorant of the reality out of which her poems were written. Going to stay with her in Mallorca was not going to Latin America, but many writers who have fled Latin America for various reasons travel to visit her. I met women there who were tortured, one in an Argentine prison.

* Forché's translation of Claribel Alegría's *Flowers from the Volcano* was published in 1982 by the University of Pittsburgh Press.

And so that world drew near to me, albeit on a nice terrace over drinks with Robert and Beryl Graves and everyone sitting around in a kind of literary salon. But, nevertheless, it was the first time I was listening to people who had been directly affected by history in some way that was palpable for me. And when I became very depressed, I thought maybe I had island fever. Claribel would sit with a drink every afternoon and wait for the mail to come, blank-eyed, sad, unreachable; I couldn't speak to her. And she would search through the mail for news of her friends or relatives, and then an hour later she would suddenly be all cheery and dressed and ready to engage in the evening. But those moments haunted me.

I kept working on the translations, but I left, very saddened. And when I came back to California and began working very intensely for Amnesty International—I was writing my letters dutifully and all that—one day up pulls this dusty white Jeep into my driveway, and out climbs this guy with two little girls and knocks on my door. Now, I had heard about this man, Leonel Gómez Vides—I'd heard about him in Spain, there were legends about him. He introduced himself to me, but I was properly terrified about Latin American strangers who purported to be this or that. He had the two little girls with him, however, so I trusted him and let him into the house. I sat him down at the kitchen table and pointed to photographs I had taken in Spain and asked him to identify various people. He was amused, and said that someone was so-and-so and someone else was the husband of so-and-so, and so on. "That's very good," he told me. "Now," he said, "how would you like to do something for Central America, since you've translated these poems and obviously have an interest?" I knew that he was associated with many humanitarian projects in El Salvador, and I thought I would be the lady in white working in the orphanage for one year who pats the little bottoms! I pictured myself that way, rather heroically. I had a Guggenheim Fellowship to write poetry, I had the year free, and I said, "Yes, I'd like to go."

So he went out to the truck, got a roll of white butcher paper and about twenty pencils, and he smoothed the paper out on the table and began to diagram and doodle and make little drawings about the Salvadoran military and the American embassy and the various components of the Salvadoran society and economic and political structures. He did this for seventy-two hours straight, with many cups of coffee, and then he would test me, he'd say, "Okay, you are this colonel and this happens and there's possibly going to be a coup, what do you do?" He made me think of every component in this scenario. And he said,

"Look, you have a dead Jesuit priest and a dead parish priest, you have forty nuns and priests expelled from the country or arrested, this is the situation, and I want you to come to Salvador to learn about it, because our country is your country's next Vietnam."

Now, you have to understand that in 1977 El Salvador did not "exist" in the United States. It was a little country the size of my thumbnail on the largest map that you could find. And "Vietnam" was a word that awakened in me an enormous complex of feelings.

My ex-husband had gone to Vietnam, as had my next-door neighbor and most of my friends in school and brothers and boyfriends and husbands of friends—they all went off to the war because we were of the class that *went* to Vietnam. And we used to listen to those songs in high school—about the Green Berets, and about pinning "silver wings on my son's chest"—we used to cry because our friends were there, and we thought they would die. But I was a *greaser,* we thought this war was right, we were very patriotic. It didn't occur to us *not* to be until I went to the university, and I was the only one among my circle of friends who did go. . . . So I *had* to know about El Salvador. And here this man was offering me an opportunity to understand something, and also he promised me that, in an odd way, I would be able to make a contribution. So how could I not agree? I knew that I was ignorant about the situation there, and that it would be a worse ignorance to refuse this offer. But most of my friends at the time thought I was absolutely crazy to go.

The poet Robert Bly recently spoke of our not being conscious of what we were (and are) doing in El Salvador. "We did it in Vietnam," he stated, "and ever since have refused to become conscious of it. It is said that a dream will repeat itself until you understand it, until you become conscious of what's there." And I have the sense that making things conscious is exactly what you've been trying to do in your poetry.

For me it's a process of understanding, a process which has not been completed and that probably can't be completed. But it certainly was startling for me to learn not only about Central America in a very immediate way but also to learn about the limitations of my understanding. Because I wasn't equipped to see or analyze the world. My perceptions were very distorted—and I'm even talking about visual perception. I would notice things in very general terms, but there were certain things I would fail to see.

THE COLONEL

What you have heard is true. I was in his house. His wife carried a tray of coffee and sugar. His daughter filed her nails, his son went out for the night. There were daily papers, pet dogs, a pistol on the cushion beside him. The moon swung bare on its black cord over the house. On the television was a cop show. It was in English. Broken bottles were embedded in the walls around the house to scoop the kneecaps from a man's legs or cut his hands to lace. On the windows there were gratings like those in liquor stores. We had dinner, rack of lamb, good wine, a gold bell was on the table for calling the maid. The maid brought green mangoes, salt, a type of bread. I was asked how I enjoyed the country. There was a brief commercial in Spanish. His wife took everything away. There was some talk then of how difficult it had become to govern. The parrot said hello on the terrace. The colonel told it to shut up, and pushed himself from the table. My friend said to me with his eyes: say nothing. The colonel returned with a sack used to bring groceries home. He spilled many human ears on the table. They were like dried peach halves. There is no other way to say this. He took one of them in his hands, shook it in our faces, dropped it into a water glass. It came alive there. I am tired of fooling around he said. As for the rights of anyone, tell your people they can go fuck themselves. He swept the ears to the floor with his arm and held the last of his wine in the air. Something for your poetry, no? he said. Some of the ears on the floor caught this scrap of his voice. Some of the ears on the floor were pressed to the ground.

I would always marvel at the wealthy women in the suburbs of San Salvador—women playing canasta all day—and I spent many hours talking to them. They did not *see* poverty, it didn't exist for them. First of all, they never went outside the capital city, but even in the city they could go through a street in a car and not see the mother who had made a nest in rubber tires for her babies. What they saw was an assembly of colors of delight, of baskets and jugs on the heads of women. Yet they were being as accurate as they could possibly be in their descriptions.

Now, as to what *I* didn't see: I was once driving past rows of cotton fields—all I could see on either side of the highway for miles was cotton fields, and it was dusty and hot, and I was rolling along thinking about something in my usual way, which is the way that has been nurtured in this country. But I didn't see *between* the rows, where there were women and children, emaciated, in a stupor, because pesticide planes had swept over and dropped chemicals all over them, and they were coughing and lethargic from those poisonous clouds . . . and also they were living out there in the middle of these fields because they had no place else to go, underneath plastic tarps, which were no protection against the pesticides. The children had no clothing and were swollen-bellied and suffering from the second- and third-degree malnutrition that I had been taught to recognize in my work at the hospital. There they were, and I hadn't seen them. I had only seen cotton and soil between cotton plants, and a hot sky—I saw the thing endlessly and aesthetically, I saw it in a certain spatial way. So I had to be *taught* to look and to remember and to think about what I was seeing.

As I was mentioning before, we Americans—and, I'm sure, this applies to many Europeans, too—tend to register perceptions without codifying them in any political, historical, or social way. There's no sense of what creates or contributes to or who benefits from a situation. And I'm not talking about a prescriptive political ideology now—that's why I included that quote by Machado in the beginning of my book, so that it might be clear that I was speaking about a *process* of understanding and not about a political conversion.

What you're saying reminds me of John Keats's notion that "poetry must work out its own salvation in a man: It cannot be matured by law and precept, but by sensation and watchfulness in itself."

Yes, I certainly don't mean to be programmatic in my writing or ever to be strident or polemical. I don't want to argue a position, rather I want to present in language the re-creation of a moment. Any judgment, any expression, even a most carefully rendered eyewitness testimony, is viewed as political if you locate that testimony in an area associated with turmoil. Whereas you can describe something in an area that's not so associated and it will be considered something else. I tried not to write about El Salvador in poetry because I thought it might be better to do so in journalistic articles. I tried not to, but I couldn't stop; the poems just came.

At the conclusion of one of your earlier poems, "What It Cost," which is about the forced migrations in Russia and Eastern Europe of members of your grandmother's generation, one reads the words of the ghosts of the dead: "Haul your language south./There are knives in your pillows./The white birds fall another month." *You've spent a lot of time in the American Southwest, and it's interesting that the first line of the first of your poems about El Salvador reads:* "We have come far south" . . . *and concludes:* ". . . That is why we feel/it is enough to listen/to the wind jostling lemons,/to dogs ticking across the terraces,/knowing that while birds and warmer weather/are forever moving north,/the cries of those who vanish/might take years to get here." *As Robert Bly, again, has said, "It isn't accidental, in a way, that El Salvador is south of us, because 'south' in the psyche means 'down.' " One can feel the heat and torpor and intensity of the South in much of your work, and I'm curious about your affinity with and gravitation toward this region which seems, in your case, to be both physical and psychic.*

I spent my entire childhood in Michigan, and I was always compelled by the North—I happen to love the winter and the snow. I was always enamored of Russia—perhaps a sort of distorted romantic version of Russia that comes from a twentieth-century reinterpretation of the nineteenth century. But when I got older my inward focus was drawn less to the familiar, and more to those things about which I was ignorant. And I wanted to go to the Southwest and be in the desert. I learned a lot during those weeks that I camped in the desert at different times in my twenties. I went there often, and that was where I became clear inside—though it does sound like a cliché. But when I was in the Mojave Desert one time, I had this experience: I was with a friend, and we didn't speak to one another for about three or four days—I mean except for absolute necessities—but we didn't make conversation, and all of a sudden I was on this rock and I heard this *ba-bum ba-bum.* I was shocked; I realized I was hearing myself, my own heart, and I felt a certain consciousness outside myself as well. It was quite a transfiguring experience for me. And after that I was very much drawn to the re-creation of it, by going back to the desert. One time when I was watching the sunset out there —you couldn't see any visible signs of mankind or civilization, there was no power grid, and there were no wires or roads or glow of lights or anything—I realized: "This is the way it was, this is the emptiness, this is the empty earth . . ." but it wasn't empty, and I didn't know what was filling it. I think that I felt the need for a replacement, a spiritual palpability to replace the Catholicism that I had intellectually rejected when I was younger. And there it was again, only it wasn't with the need for a personal or an anthropomorphic conception of God.

As far as going to El Salvador is concerned, I told you what the reasons were for that. I don't know whether there's some reason *beyond* those reasons. Until you suggested this, I didn't know it was there. But I never would have thought, when I was little, that I would feel so compelled toward that particular part of the world.

In your extraordinary long poem "Kalaloch," you describe a sexual encounter with a female stranger on a beach in the Pacific Northwest; in "To the Stranger," you present a sexual encounter with a male stranger on a train; and in your prose reverie "This Is Their Fault," you detail moments of a masochistic sexual fantasy. In all of these, there is no salaciousness but rather a simple but mysterious presentation of the life of desire.

One thing I try not to worry about in the poetry is how "I" appear. If you have a worry about what kind of appearance you're making, you'll censor yourself and will therefore diminish or reduce whatever it is that you've experienced. I made a rule for myself that I would have to be brave, and if something was embarrassing—and I'm very easily embarrassed—so what, it had to be put down, I had to write it.

After "Kalaloch" appeared, there was, briefly, a letter-writing argument in the *American Poetry Review* about whether Carolyn Forché was gay, straight, or bisexual. And I made no comment. I just thought, "Well, run with it folks, you have a good time with that one because I really don't care what you think I am" [laughing]. I thought it was a really superficial way of dealing with the poem, but it was also sort of interesting.

KALALOCH

The bleached wood massed in bone piles,
we pulled it from dark beach and built
fire in a fenced clearing.
The posts' blunt stubs sank down,
they circled and were roofed by milled
lumber dragged at one time to the coast.
We slept there.

Each morning the minus tide—
weeds flowed it like hair swimming.
The starfish gripped rock, pastel,
rough. Fish bones lay in sun.

Each noon the milk fog sank
from cloud cover, came in
our clothes and held them
tighter on us. Sea stacks
stood and disappeared.
They came back when the sun
scrubbed out the inlet.

We went down to piles to get
mussels, I made my shirt
a bowl of mussel stones, carted
them to our grate where they smoked apart.
I pulled the mussel lip bodies out,
chewed their squeak.
We went up the path for fresh water, berries.
Hardly speaking, thinking.

During low tide we crossed
to the island, climbed
its wet summit. The redfoots
and pelicans dropped for fish.
Oclets so silent fell
toward water with linked feet.

Jacynthe said little.
Long since we had spoken *Nova Scotia.*
Michigan, and knew beauty in saying nothing.
She told me about her mother
who would come at them with bread knives then
stop herself, her face emptied.

I told her about me,
never lied. At night
at times the moon floated.
We sat with arms tight
watching flames spit, snap.
On stone and sand picking up
wood shaped like a body, like a gull.

I ran barefoot not only
on beach but harsh gravels
up through the woods.
I shit easy, covered my dropping.
Some nights, no fires, we watched
sea pucker and get stabbed
by the beacon
circling on Tatoosh.

2

I stripped and spread
on the sea lip, stretched
to the slap of the foam
and the vast red dulce.
Jacynthe gripped the earth
in her fists, opened—
the boil of the tide
shuffled into her.

The beach revolved,
headlands behind us
put their pines in the sun.
Gulls turned a strong sky.
Their pained wings held,
they bit water quick, lifted.
Their looping eyes continually
measure the distance from us,
bare women who do not touch.

Rocks drowsed, holes
filled with suds from a distance.
A deep laugh bounced in my flesh
and sprayed her.

3

Flies crawled us,
Jacynthe crawled.

With her palms she
spread my calves, she
moved my heels from each other.
A woman's mouth is
not different, sand moved
wild beneath me, her long
hair wiped my legs, with women
there is sucking, the water
slops our bodies. We come
clean, our clits beat like
twins to the loons rising up.

We are awake.
Snails sprinkle our gulps.
Fish die in our grips, there is
sand in the anus of dancing.
Tatoosh Island
hardens in the distance.
We see its empty stones
sticking out of the sea again.
Jacynthe holds tinder
under fire to cook the night's wood.

If we had men I would make
milk in me simply. She is
quiet. *I like that you*
cover your teeth.

The way that poem came about was: There's a beach on the Olympic Peninsula where the land comes up into the water in rock stacks and piles and formations. There's a lot of fog, and the ocean comes over the land; it's completely glazed and the land stretches out. I guess poets automatically think archetypically. And I was thinking: "There're these two mothers, these two women—Earth and Water" . . . I don't mean to make a cult of this idea, but it seemed as if it had to be that way . . . "and they're making love." And there *was* a woman there named Jacynthe, and we *did* spend those weeks on the beach living in this little driftwood place like a couple of banshees.

Returning to the subject of masochistic fantasies, some people tend unfortunately to confuse sexual fantasies with the institutionalization of torture in police states.

133

I think many women in this culture—and I think that it's pretty well documented—imaginatively translate their experiences of childhood and develop masochism. I think most women confront that and that they are repelled by it or do battle with it. But many women whom I've spoken with do have this problem of eroticizing their oppression. Occasionally, however, there's a replay of this kind of fantasy when discussing human rights abuses that has nothing to do with the reality of torture, imprisonment, and assassination. It's what an inexperienced mind does with an abstraction that it has eroticized on another level in the light of its own culture.

When I was at a congress on human rights in Canada not long ago, there was an interesting discussion about this subject, and I expressed how horrified I was about this confusion. And a writer began saying, "Oh, surely you're not such a prude that you don't enjoy it!" And he started to talk in this chic, hip way about kinky sex. But another writer, Hans Magnus Enzensberger, whom I have high regard for, said, "She isn't talking about your little trips; there's a big difference between your little sexual parlor games and the reality of torture."

But if you're even willing to say: "I had certain masochistic fantasies as a child that I later, to my own horror, saw the reality of somewhere" . . . and if you're willing to acknowledge the complexity and admit that, for example, altruistic work isn't always simple, and to portray yourself as one of the people for whom it's not simple—*that*, then, is what's important. And it's also important to see within ourselves first every manifestation of atrocity. The Holocaust didn't occur because only the *Germans* were somehow peculiar and that therefore something like that couldn't happen again. We have to confront this now.

It must have been terrifying to confront the violent realities in El Salvador.

I was very close to Monsignor Oscar Romero just before he was killed. And I had a close brush with death: I was with a young defecting member of the Christian Democratic Party, and we confronted a death squad that had three machine guns trained on our windshield. They had enough time to kill us, but this young man had an uncanny quickness of reflexes, and he managed to throw the car into reverse and floor it and get back through a walled gate. But though it was split-second, I had enough time to see the machine guns. There's no reason why I'm here. Functionally, it was just a fluke. No one who was close to that particular episode—including the young man's sister—understands why we survived it. There was something holding them back. We suspect that they weren't quite expecting us at that time. But at any rate, they fled.

It might have turned into another **Missing.**

It was difficult for me to watch that film. It brought back a lot for me. And it made me realize that if the young Mr. Horman had the kinds of friends I had in El Salvador, he might have survived. I realize that I came close, but . . . first of all, I was blessed by fate, and second, I did have many Salvadorans who were very willing to take serious risks on my behalf. Many women. About a week before the incident with the death squad I just described to you, actually, I was chased by them as I was driving with a woman—who drove like a mad person, in order to save our lives—around the road that circles Catholic University. And she said to me, during the chase, what was going to happen. And she was very calm. I felt very afraid, but you can't afford to give in to it at the time or you won't survive. Now, of course, it's an unreality because it's recollected in the past . . . and I can never re-create those moments. Right after, though, when I knew I was saved, I would shake for a little while and then pull myself together again. . . . But, see, this is something that I lived for a short period that the people down there live every day!

What were you like when you returned to this country?

I was thin, I had four different strains of dysentery, and I could not shut up about El Salvador. I was not only hopelessly obsessed with the subject when I was talking to my friends, but I also tried to write about it, unsuccessfully for a while, and then wasn't able to get anything in print when I did. Some of the publications that I approached even thought that I was making it all up because I wasn't a credentialed journalist.

Did you ever feel that you had come too close to the edge?

I could have, though I didn't lose my sanity even briefly. I became very lucid, but I knew what was going to happen. And I felt more and more powerless to do anything about it, because no one would listen to me. And I began to realize that it wouldn't matter if they did. I had to experience the full impact of this horror, that this is indeed what happened in Vietnam . . . and that I couldn't stop it. And that I was going to have to see it almost like someone whose eyelids are held open and who can't stop looking at something. And it was very hard to get through that period.

One of the things that's very heartening is that I met a whole network of people—many of them journalists—who never went off the path; who got involved during the Vietnam period for whatever reasons and did whatever they could, however effectually or ineffectually; who didn't go and climb the corporate ladder; who have insisted that their work be subservient to their conscience. There's a whole group of people like this in Washington, D.C., who were gathered together the other night. And we learned that, even though we all look very different now, we're all roughly the same age and had the same formative experiences during the late sixties . . . and we're doing the same things at the moment—pulling the lid off chemical wastes or finding out about what happened to Karen Silkwood or whatever.

Walt Whitman wrote: "The attitude of great poets is to cheer up slaves and horrify despots."

That's an interesting view. I don't want to think of everyone who's been horrified as a despot, because a lot of people who have been horrified are very good-hearted and well-intentioned, especially the young ones. They come and they say, "What should we do?" They think that to write in an engaged way means you have to go to exotic climes. People don't want to learn about what is in their own immediate sphere. And this is understandable, isn't it, because of all the duplicity. "What should we do?" "That's not the beginning," I have to say. "Set off now, and find *out* what you should do. The answer is not the beginning. The answer is, maybe, at the end, if you're very lucky."

[New York City, 1982]

Sam Shepard

THE THEATER CRITIC MICHAEL FEINGOLD ONCE REMARKED THAT the paradox of Sam Shepard consisted in his having "the mind of a Kafka trapped in the body of a Jimmy Stewart."

It was Franz Kafka who wrote that "A book must be the axe for the frozen sea in us." And in the more than forty plays that Sam Shepard has written since 1964, this playwright has been breaking open that frozen sea with an originality of vision, a jolting intermingling of humor and grief, a profound examination of the hopes and failures of the American family and the American Dream, and an astonishing ear for the rhythmic cadences of the American idiom. With plays like *The Unseen Hand, Curse of the Starving Class, Buried Child* (for which he won the 1979 Pulitzer Prize), *True West, Fool for Love,* and *A Lie of the Mind,* Shepard has cloaked himself with the mantle once worn by Eugene O'Neill and Tennessee Williams.

Early on in his career, Sam Shepard wrote: "I love horse racing and stock cars. I love the Rolling Stones. I love Brigitte Bardot. I love Marlon Brando and James Dean and Stan Laurel and Otis Redding and Wilson Pickett and Jimmie Rodgers and Bob Dylan and the Who and Jesse James and Crazy Horse and the Big Bopper and Nina Simone and Jackson Pollock and Muhammad Ali and Emile Griffith. . . ." And he once tried to describe himself—and, in fact, much of his super-energized, music-driven, demon-obsessed early work—with a few of his "favorite words," among them: "Coyote, Crow, Choctaw, Gris Gris, Mojo, Cheyenne, Sycamore, Ghost, Saint, Aztec, Messiah, Tootsie Roll, Antelope, Python, Moxie, Hooch, Wolf, Pine, Pistol, Abalone, Cowboy, Stranger."

This Franz Kafka with a lariat, this desert-haunted cowboy/stranger, has also, as an actor, attained the popularity of matinee idols such as Jimmy Stewart or Gary Cooper. With his lean, lanky, cleft-chinned, high-cheekboned, snaggletoothed, blue-eyed good looks, Sam Shepard has been a magnetic presence in films such as *Days of Heaven, Resurrec-*

tion, Frances, The Right Stuff, Country, Fool for Love, and *Crimes of the Heart.* In the words of *The Right Stuff* director Phil Kaufman: "[Shepard] has a quality that is so rare now—you don't see it in the streets much, let alone in the movies—a kind of bygone quality of the forties when guys could wear leather jackets and be laconic and still say a lot without verbally saying anything. Most of the great actors of our time tend to be the urban types who are verbal and have a high energy that transmits what they're trying to say, whether it's [Dustin] Hoffman or [Al] Pacino or [Robert] De Niro. Sam is more laid-back, like Gary Cooper." To which Shepard once characteristically stated: "They told me for this movie my model would be Gary Cooper. I don't know how to take that. I could never connect with Gary Cooper. When I think of a rugged individualist, I right away think of Stan Laurel. Out of all the silent comics, he sort of sticks out in my mind as the truest and also the funniest."

In his subtle and brilliant journal, *Rolling Thunder Logbook,* which recounts and reflects on his on-the-road adventures during Bob Dylan's 1975 rock and roll tour, Shepard writes: "If mystery is solved, the case is dropped. In this case, in the case of Dylan, the mystery is never solved, so the case keeps on. It keeps coming up again. Over and over the years. Who is this character anyway?" And one could ask the same question about Sam Shepard himself.

Born Samuel Shepard Rogers III on November 5, 1943, in Fort Sheridan, Illinois, Shepard was an army brat whose family was stationed for various periods in South Dakota, Utah, Florida, and Guam, and finally settled down on an avocado ranch in Duarte, California—an end-of-the-road valley town east of Los Angeles. At nineteen, he left his family and came to New York City as an aspiring actor/musician, started writing his exuberant early plays, and later moved to London with his actress-wife O-Lan and son Jesse. He then returned to northern California and, eventually, to a ranch in Santa Fe and a farm in Virginia, where he has lived with actress Jessica Lange, their daughter Hanna, and Lange's daughter Alexandra.

Like Bob Dylan, whom he resembles in many ways, Sam Shepard is an intensely private person who shies away from journalists, preferring to allow transformed glimpses of himself to appear in his plays and in books like *Hawk Moon* and the wonderful *Motel Chronicles*—collections of poems/meditations/dreams/journals/visions. (Don Shewey's recent biography, *Sam Shepard,* gives an insightful view of the playwright's life, and particularly of his complicated, shattered relationship with his alcoholic father.)

In conversation, Sam Shepard is happy to speak directly about things that concern him, and indirectly (or not at all) about issues of superficial or "merely personal" importance. With an undeniably engaging blue-eyed squint and a kind of Western-Swing twang to his voice, he continually displays an unnerving, surprising, and charmingly boyish sense of humor. But most disarming of all is the way he unhesitatingly confronts, explores, and clarifies the most painful and sorrowful of matters—loss, separation, disillusion, powerlessness, weakness, fear, lies.

Kafka said: "A lie is often an expression of the fear that one may be crushed by the truth. It is a projection of one's own littleness, of the sin of which one is afraid." And in his most recent play, *A Lie of the Mind*. Sam Shepard has made his most fearless, controlled, and deepest penetration into the realm of the American psyche. For in this story of two American families—with its revelation and reconciliation of the relationships between and among a violent son, his battered wife, and his angelic brother—the playwright shows how personal and social dreams and lies are one and the same, as he creates—as he once said Bob Dylan created—"a mythic atmosphere out of the land around us. The land we walk on every day and never see until someone shows it to us."

In December of 1985, Shepard directed the New York premiere of his three-hour-and-forty-five-minute masterpiece in a simple but visionary production that featured a cast of actors including Amanda Plummer, Harvey Keitel, Geraldine Page, Aidan Quinn, and Will Patton, as well as the live old-timey music of the Red Clay Ramblers, who performed songs of Skip James, Lefty Frizzell, and Stephen Foster, among others.

And it was in an appropriately old-fashioned, unassuming drugstore on Cañon Drive in Beverly Hills—one of Shepard's favorite "reading" haunts—and in the tea room of the Chateau Marmont hotel in Hollywood that the following interview took place in April 1986.

Maybe I should make a fire. Would you like a fire? I'll make a fire.

Maybe I should rip up the Sunday Paper into tiny pieces and try not to get hung up on the ads.

Maybe I should finish digging the hole I was digging in the backyard.

Maybe I should make a cup of tea and take Vitamin C. Would you like a cup of tea?

Maybe I should just take a walk with no destination.

Maybe I should stay in one place and
stay put and stop making up reasons to move.

Maybe we could both have a conversation.
Would you like to have a conversation?*

*   *   *

*In many of your plays, your characters talk a lot about and often per-
form music on stage; and the "feel" of your plays is often that of a jazz
improvisation or an extended country, blues, or rock and roll song.
When did your preoccupation with music begin?*

My dad was a kind of semiprofessional, Dixieland-type drummer, and I
learned the drums from him. When I was about twelve, we bought our
first Ludwig drum set from a pawnshop—a marching-band bass drum,
great big tom-toms, and big, deep snaredrum. We stripped the paint off
of them, varnished them, and then set them out in the orchard to dry.

I was in high school in Duarte, way out in the valley [east of Los
Angeles], and started playing in a band called Nat's Cats. Nat played
the clarinet, another guy played the trumpet, and I played drums. And
we performed old Swing music, kind of Dixieland stuff, and gradually
moved into rock and roll. Trumpet, clarinet, drums—that was the trio.
And I remember that the trumpet player was this really odd guy. Back
in the fifties, you could order wild animals through the mail—it was
legal in those days. And in this guy's backyard he had alligators and
wolves; and when we'd go rehearse over there, there'd be all these
strange animals wandering all around.

Oddly enough, in this same weird little high school that I went to,
there was a student named Mike Romero, who also played the drums.
So this competition started—a kind of drum wars!—and I once went
over to his place and stayed up all night and listened to jazz records for
the first time. Then we played for hours, and I discovered what the left
hand could do—letting the drum hand ride—because a rock and roll
drummer would turn the hand over and smash the snare drum, while
the jazz drummer would hold the stick in his open palm so that he could
get this *snap* out of it. Mike Romero was the guy who turned me on to
that, and all of a sudden the drums opened up for me. And when I
moved to New York City in 1963, I started playing drums for the Holy
Modal Rounders.

* (from *Motel Chronicles.* © 1982 by Sam Shepard)

I've always felt a great affinity with music. I've felt myself to be more of a musician than anything else. I'm not proficient on any one instrument. But I think I have a musical sense of things . . . and writing seems to me to be a musical experience—rhythmically and in many other ways. But I don't think that that's so unusual: Most of the old guys had the same sense—Christopher Marlowe thought of himself as a musician. Just another musician killed at a bar [laughing]. . . . And there's that theory that he was Shakespeare.

One of your fans told me that you were Shakespeare. And like you, Shakespeare didn't go around promoting himself in the media!

I think that's because he didn't exist. I think there was a whole cover-up for him.

You do?

Yeah. I think there's a big mystery about Shakespeare, but it's too late to confirm it [laughing]. I mean, look at the plays, the way they suddenly shift gears—from the earlier period to those later tragedies. Something happened that nobody knows about. I think he was involved in something deeply mysterious and esoteric, and at the time they had to keep it under wraps. There's an awful lot of amazing insight in his plays that doesn't come from an ordinary mind. And there was a tremendous monastic movement at that time. Who knows what he was into?

And Shakespeare didn't mince words either. "To be or not to be" is right to the point [laughing]. You can't get much more to the point than that. That *is* the question. Are you going to be here or not? What's the deal? Are you going to be or not be?

When did you make that decision?

Well, you decide that every day.

Do you sometimes wake up and wonder about it?

For me it's been a process of overcoming a tremendous morning despair. It's been diminishing over the years. But I still feel a trace of this thing that I can't really track down.

143

Some people are just "up and at 'em!"

I've tried desperately to be like that, six A.M. and bang!—feed the horses and milk the goats. I used to work a lot on ranches where I grew up, and I had to rise at five-thirty in the morning. In fact there's something healthy about going against the grain of the laziness of the body.

In a prose poem you once wrote called "Rhythm," you make it sound as if everything *is rhythm: "Oilcan rhythms, ratchet wrench rhythms. Playing cards in bicycle spokes . . . Water slapping rocks. Flesh slapping flesh. Boxing rhythms. Racing rhythms. Rushing brooks. . . ."*

Well, it is, pretty much. But there's that distinction between tempo and rhythm, where tempo is a man-made invention. . . . In San Francisco, I once studied with an African drummer named Kwaku Dadey, who had been playing since he was seven years old in Ghana. I'd always thought that polyrhythm was an invention of contemporary jazz, but it turns out that it's an ancient African concept. And I remember that one day about eight of us got together to play congas: We played in rhythms of fives and sixes and in six-eight, three-four, and four-four time simultaneously. Everything stacked and piled up, and you had to carry some of the lines three or four measures to catch up, but eventually it all worked out—it was hard to believe!

There was no connecting principle?

Of course there was. Like the *ocean*. If *you're* playing an individual part and *I'm* playing an independent part and we can't figure out how these two are going to merge—assuming you're sticking to your part and I to mine—they just eventually merge. I don't know how. But the rhythmic structures underneath each one of these parts all somehow map out. And what's the principle of that? It's way beyond music. . . . That man was an amazing teacher, with an understanding of the crossroads and of how everything fits together. I learned a lot from him.

Like Chuck Berry's "Johnny B. Goode"—"Strumming with the rhythm that the drivers made."

Lyrically, Chuck Berry works off rhythm, that's all there is to it. He's got an unbelievably rhythmic sense of words. Nobody writes like that. . . . Maybe Hank Williams, but in a different, simpler way.

144

When I see your plays, I'm sometimes reminded of some of the songs written by the Band.

I love Levon Helm, he's one of my favorite guys. You know, Levon once shot himself in the leg while practicing his quick draw! [laughing] And there's another guy Levon once told me about who shot his nuts off—another drummer, by the way—and Levon said that he's never played the same since [laughing]. Oh, boy! Carrying a .45 in your crotch when you're playing the drums is really asking for trouble!

Do you know the Band's song called "Daniel and the Sacred Harp," which tells the story of a guy who buys a magical instrument that he has no rights to; and while he's playing his heart out on it in a meadow, he notices that he's lost his shadow—perhaps his soul?

A bad sign. You know *Dr. Faustus* by Christopher Marlowe? I'd love to make a film of that sometime. I even prefer it to Goethe's version because of Marlowe's incredible language.

When did you first read the plays of Marlowe?

I'll tell you: Aside from assigned reading in high school, I didn't read any plays except for a couple of Brecht things when I was living in New York City. I avoided reading out of arrogance, really. But when I went to England in the early seventies, I suddenly found myself having a kind of dry spell. It was difficult for me to write, so I started to read. And I read most of the Greek guys—Aeschylus, Sophocles—I studied up on those guys, and I'm glad I did. I was just amazed by the simplicity of the ancient Greek plays, for instance—they were dead simple. Nothing complex or tricky . . . which surprised the hell out of me, because I'd assumed they were beyond me. But now I began to comprehend what they were talking about, and they turned out to be accessible.

They're a lot about the family romance, aren't they?

They're all about destiny! That's the most powerful thing. Everything is foreseen, and we just play it out. Like Oedipus . . . the thing is laid down, and there's nothing he can do about it.

You don't think a person can shape his own destiny?

Oh, maybe. But first you have to know what your destiny is.

When did you think you knew your own?

I'm not so sure I do. I'm not saying I know my destiny, I'm saying that it exists. It exists, and it can become a duty to discover it. Or it can be shirked. But if you take it on as your duty, then it becomes a different thing from dismissing it altogether and just imagining that it'll work itself out anyway. I mean, it will. But it's more interesting to try to find it and know it.

It's been said that if you truly live out your destiny you can create a Diamond Body—an imperishable substance that can outlive your personal death.

There's a thing called the Necklace of the Buddha. These ancient Tibetan lamas developed a substance through meditation that was deposited in the bones—right in the back of the neck, like calcium deposits. And on their deaths, this substance was extracted and was given to others who were then able to have contact with the dead priests: There was something in those bones that actually transmitted something of the beings who had died. Now, that's a highly evolved practice, and I don't think we have anything in this culture that's quite like that.

In your play Suicide in B♭, *Niles says: "I wonder where my voice is." And in your play* The Mad Dog Blues, *Kosmo says: "I want my band. I don't want a dozen bands. I just wanna' play my music. My own special music." You seem to have found your own voice, on the outskirts of Duarte, all on your own.*

You know, Duarte was a weird accumulation of things—a strange kind of melting pot: Spanish, Okie, black, Midwestern elements all jumbled together. People on the move who couldn't move anymore, who wound up in trailer camps. And my grandmother—my father's mother —was part something . . . maybe American Indian, I'm not sure what. She was real dark with black eyes, and I don't know what that was all about—there was a cover-up somewhere back there.

And as far as my "voice" goes, I'm not so sure it's "mine." I had a sense that a voice existed that needed expression, that there was a voice that wasn't being *voiced,* if you want to put it like that. But is it "mine"?

Your early plays seem to have a certain "style," which is a different thing from a "voice."

It is. Style is the outer trappings. And *voice* is even different from language, which is a manifestation of something. But a "voice" is almost without words . . . it's something in the spaces, in between.

What was the first thing you ever wrote?

I remember that when I was a kid I wrote a story about a Coke bottle. You know that, in the old days, Coke bottles had the name of the city where they were manufactured inscribed on the bottom—St. Paul, Dubuque, wherever. So I wrote this story about this bottle and its travels. It would get filled up in one town, someone would drink it and throw it out the window, and then it would get on a truck and go somewhere else. . . . It was one of those Coke bottle stories [laughing].

In Suicide in B♭, *Niles says: "I'm afraid to be lonely. . . . That's the reason I invented music. It filled me up. I got so filled that I couldn't go on. Now I gotta start over."*

Yeah. There it is. Starting over.

Your most recent play, A Lie of the Mind, *though, seems like a real bringing together and transformation of many of your oldest and deepest "voices."*

That's twenty-one years of work there. It was a tough play to write because I had the first act very clearly in mind, then went off on a tangent and had to throw away two acts and start again. And then it began to tell itself. Like a story you've heard a long time ago that's now come back.

A writer once stated: "In the areas with which we are concerned, insight only occurs as a lightning bolt. The text is the thunder peal rolling long behind."

Did I write that? [laughing]

No, the critic Walter Benjamin did. What was the lightning bolt for A Lie of the Mind?

147

The incredible schism between a man and a woman in which something is broken in a way that almost kills the thing that was causing them to be together. The devastating break—that was the lightning bolt.

But isn't it this lightning bolt that woke them up? It seems as if Beth, the battered, brain-damaged wife who appears to be crazy and living in a dream world, is in fact the clearest-seeing person in the play.

Yes, she's the most sensitive. I've had a couple of experiences of people very close to me who suffered brain damage and who underwent surgery. And the most startling thing in both of these cases was the sense of one's own helplessness in relation to what these two people were going through because of the innocence of their states. We use words all the time; we take them for granted, and suddenly you're faced with people who have no language . . . it's gone. And you become aware that language is a learned function—it's an obvious fact—but at that moment you truly become aware of it when you realize that it can be lost. Those people are on the open end of the stick, they're vulnerable and alive to the fact of language . . . while we're dead to it. We usually don't understand how it affects people and what kind of luxury it is to have language. So it shakes you up.

You once wrote a work entitled Inacoma. *What was that about?*

It was an improvisational collaboration, and it was based on the story of Karen Ann Quinlan—one of the first pull-the-plug cases. What's always fascinated me is how the living have to deal with the near-dead or with those who are in that territory, how they have to adjust *their* world to fit the other one. You know, in brain damage, there's no definite knowledge about the psychic position of the person in that condition. Again, it has to do with degrees. Someone can be alive in one area of the brain and shut off in another part . . . and you don't always know which is which.

It's extraordinarily moving when Beth, pointing to her head, says: "This is me. This is me now. The way I am. Now. This. All different. I —I live inside this. Remember. Remembering."

It's interesting how you can be lost in an area like memory—memory is very easy to get lost in. Some things can't get lost, though, because there they're based on *emotional* memory, which is a different thing from just trying to remember the name of a person or some fact. But to remember where you were touched has more of a reverberation. It remembers itself to you.

Beth seems to have been touched in her heart. And I've recently been reading a lot about this California high school girl, suffering from severe heart disease, whose schoolmate decided to will her his own heart. And suddenly he died—as if he had willed his own death, too—and she now has his transplanted heart inside of her!

It's an amazing story. He contracted something real quick . . . and it does sound as if he willed it. . . . Love can do funny things.

It does funny things to Eddie and May in Fool for Love—*two lovers who are also half-brother and half-sister. In his song "Oh, Sister"— which might have been written specifically for these two characters— Bob Dylan sings: "Oh, sister, when I come to lie in your arms/You should not treat me like a stranger./Our Father would not like the way that you act/And you must realize the danger." The "Father" in your play is called "The Old Man"; and just as his children embrace before they split apart forever, he yells out to his son: "You two can't come together! You gotta' hold my end a' this deal. I got nobody now. Nobody! You can't betray me!"—as if he doesn't want his children/lovers/fantasies to be together.*

From his point of view, there's a danger of wholeness. Once they become whole, it shatters his entire existence, which depends on being split. . . . But there are a lot of different ways of looking at it.

The Bible says that what happens to the parents is a sign of what will happen to the children.

"The gods visit the sins of the fathers upon the children." . . . Yeh, that's what happened.

Ever since Cain and Abel's parents got kicked out of the garden.

Ever since World War II! [laughing] Actually, all the way back to Egypt. That Egyptian myth of the god Osiris and his brother Set, who cut him

into pieces, and Osiris' sister/wife Isis—that has a lot to do with Dylan's
"Oh, Sister" and "Isis," too. Those two songs really got to me when I
first heard him sing them during the Rolling Thunder tour—there was a
mystical thing going on when he performed them. And that Egyptian
myth is fantastic . . . Isis finding one piece of Osiris' dismembered
body here, another piece there, and slowly rejoining them. And then
there's something about a bird telling Isis that the body's buried in a
tree—the American Indians also buried their dead in trees to keep the
coyotes away from the corpses. And beyond the actual physical restor-
ing of Osiris is the bringing together of the emotional, psychological,
and intellectual aspects—not just the arms and legs but the whole
works! I used a lot of ancient Egyptian stuff in Beth's speeches in *A Lie
of the Mind.*

At the beginning of **A Lie of the Mind,** *Jake's talking to his brother
Frankie on the phone, and the latter says: "Jake! Don't do that! You're
gonna' disconnect us again." And you can notice how the word* disconnect *and, later, a word like* remember *almost act as ritualistic words
in the play. Yet the words also pass by unnoticed because they're so well
rooted in intense but simple colloquial speech.*

I think you have to start in that colloquial territory, and from there
move on and arrive in poetic country . . . but not the other way
around. I've noticed that even with the Greek guys, especially with
Sophocles, there's a very simple, rawboned language. The choruses are
"poetic," but the speech of the characters themselves is terse, cut to the
bone, and pointed to the heart of the problem. It's like Merle Haggard
tunes like "My Own Kind of Hat"—I do this, that, and some other
thing, but I wear my own kind of hat. . . . Real simple.

*A wisdom teacher once said that the most difficult barrier in one's life is
the conquest of lying—lies of the mind.*

But how do you come to see that? It's a hard pill to swallow that
everything is a lie. Everything . . . even the truth! But if you even begin
to approach that awareness, then something new takes place, because
you start to see that there's another dimension of a relationship between
yourself and the truth—the *real* truth as opposed to the real lies. Because everything, in a way, is suggestion: I suggest to myself that I'm
brave, though it turns out that I'm a coward. But the suggestion is so

powerful that I believe it, even in the face of my cowardice. The truth is that we can't face the truth.

But if you act bravely, even though you're a coward, then maybe you are brave.

One part of you might be like a lion, but another part might be like a mouse. We don't understand the different parts of ourselves: My body might be very brave, but my emotions might be cowardly. And it seems to me that the first step is to find out which is which. Because if you go off believing that one part is strong and it's actually weak, you're going to be in for a shock!

As when Jake beats his wife up.

The shock of that kind of violence *brings* something. I'm not in any way suggesting that violence is a way of catharsis—I don't believe that at all. Nor do I believe that acting out one's anger is necessarily going to clean you of it; if anything, it may just provoke more anger. But that kind of accidental confrontation, especially between men and women, can bring about—even if only temporarily—a kind of awakening. Because a man can believe himself to be in control of his emotions, yet in a flash of an eye he can lose it, totally, and be shocked into seeing what he's really made of. . . . But to get into that kind of thing with a woman is a cowardly act. And if he's a man at all and doesn't see that, there's no way he can be truthful with himself.

Doesn't Jake, by wounding Beth, make both him and her wake up?

But they wake up into a lostness. They're not *found* in that state—it's not like, "Oh, now I realize my situation and I know where to turn." It's a lostness. Lostness can be profoundly rejuvenating in a way—it's a desperate time and full of despair and all that—but being *really* lost can start something that's brand new. Now, there are different kinds of lostness—you can be lost and not know what street you're on; you can be lost emotionally; you can be lost with other people; you can be lost in yourself. I think you continually turn around that circle—finding yourself lost and then getting relatively found.

To me, writing is a way of bringing things back together a little bit. If I can at least write something, I start to feel that I'm gathering out of that lostness something that has some kind of structure and form, and something that, one hopes, can be translated to others. I don't know if you can ever get *totally* found—I've met people who are convinced that they know what direction they're going in, and they seem to be very together. But maybe they're believing in a lie . . . a belief in a lie can be very powerful. And then again, maybe some of it's true . . . who's to say? When I was acting in *Resurrection,* I went to a lot of charismatic churches where they lay on hands and everything . . . and boy, you'd be hard-pressed to argue with somebody and say that he or she hadn't *really* found Jesus! They'd certainly found something . . . whether it was Jesus Christ or an emotional truth or whatever. Whether it was true or not is another story.

Some of your characters do seem to have staked a legitimate claim in the realm of truth. Beth, for instance. And in Motel Chronicles *you describe a little girl "chasing a tiny piece of cellophane blowing across a vacant lot . . . speaking to the cellophane as though it was a being of the wind," a girl who "feels no separation between herself and the cellophane. Both being blown. Both being together in the same moment."*

And they're the hardest ones to say anything about. It's much easier to define something that's bent and go with the way it's misshapen. But to define or give an impression of something or someone that's clean like that little girl is very difficult. We're not whole, we're in pieces most of the time, the mind is distracted.

You know, there's a great yearning to get back to that state, and there are all sorts of methods that have been developed for that purpose. I was just talking to an old friend of mine who's having a nervous breakdown—the last person in the world I ever thought would be in that state. And he told me that he was thinking of going on a "vision quest." There's apparently a vision quest cult based on the American Indian practice of going off for three days by yourself. And I said that that was great if it could serve the purpose of confronting the essentials. But I think it's incredibly difficult to do that today. If it happens accidentally, as it apparently did to Werner Erhardt . . . well, then, he's a lucky man. But is that an excuse for starting an entire organization based on his personal breakthrough? I don't know. . . . And I think that the question of death—of trying to take a truthful look at it—is missing in a lot of people's activities today. The health movement and jogging movement sometimes seem to me to reflect an incredible yearning to escape death—this fanatical thing of running to build up the body!

In his recent biography of you, the journalist and theater critic Don Shewey, who obviously greatly admires your work, makes several comments about your own supposed "macho" image.

Just because machismo exists, doesn't mean that it *shouldn't* exist. There's this attitude today that certain antagonistic forces have to be ignored or completely shut out rather than entered into in order to explore and get to the heart of them. All you have to do is enter one rodeo event to find out what that's all about . . . and you find out *fast* —in about eight seconds! So rather than avoid the issue, why not take a dive into it? I'm not saying whether it's good or bad—I think that the moralistic approach to these notions is stupid. It's not a "moral" issue, it's an issue of existence. Machismo may be an evil force . . . but what in fact is it?

I knew this guy down in the Yucatán who was so macho he decided to demonstrate to this princess he saw on the beach how *powerfully* he could swim. So he swam out into the ocean, got caught in the current, and drowned himself. Now, *he* found out *fast*. What was that moment like when he suddenly realized that because of his vanity he was going to die? I know what this thing is about because I was a victim of it, it was a part of my life, my old man tried to force on me a notion of what it was to be a "man." And it destroyed my dad. But you can't avoid facing it.

That guy who went swimming sounds foolhardy rather than evil or courageous.

It was crazy. At the moment he entered the water he thought he was a man. But he was taken by the ocean—for the sake of showing off to this girl. And he flat died. He was dead.

A sacrifice to the goddess!

Yeh. But I don't think the goddess knew what was going on at all . . . she just walked off the beach.

At the end of your play The Unseen Hand, *an old Wild West gunfighter, who's been brought back to life by Willie the Space Freak, reflects: "A man's gotta' be still long enough to figure out his next move. Know what I mean? Like in checkers, fer example. Can't just plunge in. Gotta' make plans. Figure out yer moves. . . . That's the great thing about this country, ya' know. The fact that you can make yer own moves in yer own time without some guy behind the scenes pullin' the switches on ya'." And it's interesting that the American pioneer myth and the spiritual mission and yearning you were talking about are often spoken of in exactly the same way. There seems to be a connection between these two things, such that True West equals True East!*

It's very strong, the connection between physical territory and inner territory. In America we've run out of the former; and even though they talk about going to the moon and the planets as being an extension of that, it's going to wind up at the same borderline. Now, the spiritual notion talks about something that's more hopeful, in a way, because the inner search doesn't come to some Pacific Ocean where it just builds Los Angeles—it's a never-ending process. But it seems to me that there could be a real meeting between a true Western—meaning "Western Hemisphere"—spirit and the inner one . . . and it doesn't have to remain on the level of being courageous with the land anymore. The land's been discovered. There's a different kind of courage that's being called for now. A brand new kind of courage.

The poet William Carlos Williams once wrote: "The pure products of America/go crazy—." And some critics have seen your plays be about these kinds of "real," indigenous, almost overly interbred Americans— now fragmented and deracinated.

I don't know. Insanity is something you're up against all the time. You always have to grapple with that. It's much easier to go crazy than to stay sane. Much easier. Insanity's the easy way out.

What about those questions you ask about America in Rolling Thunder Logbook: *"How did we arrive where we are now? What series of events actually went down to cause us to be at this point in time? Where exactly are we? On the road to our dinner in a plastic hotel."*

They're questions and not necessarily answerable. Some questions are much more powerful than the answers.

In your plays, when you write about the family, one ineluctably senses the social world; and when you write about the social world, one feels the personal.

That's the kind of situation we're all dealing with now—the sense of being moved beyond our recognition. Where is this thing taking us—this incredible, rapid demise, individually and collectively? And a lot of different people have different answers—political, psychological, spiritual. But apparently no one's come across *the* answer, because the situation's still moving. So the thing is to stand in front of it—and face it. Something's moving us at a really fast rate. It's an amazing time, and you do what you can. You have to know that you should be *here* instead of *there;* you have to find your role, and then go ahead and play it. And maybe someone's role is to fight against insanity, because the influences of insanity are ubiquitous now—everything's trying to drive us nuts.

In your early writings, one finds a lot of harrowing depictions of demonic states and possession trances.

In those days I had a lot of emotional earthquakes that I didn't understand because I was in the grips of them. I didn't realize even *that* much . . . I was just running wild with them and didn't know where they were taking me.

*In your recent work—*Fool for Love, A Lie of the Mind—*however, you've been clearly and consciously entering right into the earthquake zone.*

I had no choice. At a certain point you've got to do that, otherwise you end up writing diddlybop plays. Now, the ear of the typical "psychological" play doesn't have any reverberation anymore. Plays have to go beyond just "working out problems"—that's not the thing I'm talking about. What makes O'Neill's *Long Day's Journey into Night* such a great work, for instance, is that O'Neill moves past his own personal family situation into a much wider dimension. I read that play in high school, and I've always thought that that was truly the great American play. It's so overwhelmingly honest—O'Neill just doesn't pull any punches. You can't confront that play without being moved.

It's been said, with regard to that work, that children often live out the unconscious and fantasy lives of their parents.

Yes, but certain things that occur inside the family often leave marks on the emotional life that are far *stronger* than fantasy. What might be seen as the "fantasy" is, to me, just a kind of rumination on those deep marks, a manifestation of the emotional and psychological elements Sometimes in someone's gesture you can notice how a parent is somehow inhabiting that person without there being any awareness of that. How often are you aware that a gesture is coming from your old man? Sometimes you can look at your hand and see your father. But it's a complex scheme, it's not that easy to pinpoint. Again, the thing is not to avoid the issue but to see that it exists.

I gather that it was also when you were in high school that you discovered Beckett's Waiting for Godot.

Yeh, I came across it accidentally, and I'd never seen anything like *that* before.

That play really is like a piece of music.

Beckett's like Little Richard and Jimi Hendrix combined! [laughing] He's a fantastic musician. Of course, he was James Joyce's secretary, and the two of them used to sing together. Joyce would sit around and sing ballads—a real balladeer!

Thinking of your brain-damaged character Beth in A Lie of the Mind *and of the deeply musical way she has of expressing herself, I recall a statement by the German poet Novalis that goes: "Every disease is a musical problem, every cure a musical solution."*

To me, music *and* humor are both very healing. I once heard about a guy who'd contracted some strange terminal illness; no one could figure it out, and he was diminishing day by day. So he locked himself in a motel room and just watched all the Marx Brothers movies and injected himself intravenously with vitamin C. And in a week, the disease had reversed itself . . . and he's still alive today!

Linus Pauling would have said it was the vitamin C that did the trick. You think it's the Marx Brothers.

Maybe it was reciprocal [laughing]. . . . But that's the trouble with modern rock and roll, by the way: It's lost its sense of humor. It's become so morbidly stylistic and sour—there's no joy in it. And I think it's disastrous that a genuine sense of humor has been smothered.

When do you think the smothering began?

It began with the Doors! [laughing] The Doors had *no* sense of humor —they were *grim*. Now, I knew Jim Morrison for a little while, and in fact he *did* have a sense of humor—a bizarre one—but he never really exhibited it onstage.

You know, there's that myth that Jim Morrison isn't really dead and buried in Paris but that someone took his place. . . . Jesse James, the same thing. In the sixties in some hospital in Florida, this guy claimed to be the original Jesse James. He was 110 years old and he had all the bullet holes in his legs in all of the supposedly same places; and he had a black cook who was 109 years old who *also* had wounds and stuff. And they told these stories about their past . . . and then they died [laughing].

You're not claiming you're the real Jim Morrison!

I do not claim to be Jim Morrison! [laughing]

So what musicians do you like to listen to right now?

Billy Joe Royal, Ricky Skaggs, Stevie Ray Vaughan, Lou Ann Barton, the Blasters. I guess what I like is mostly country and western or else stuff that has a real blues feel to it. As far as straight up-and-down rock and roll goes, I don't think there's hardly anybody worth shaking a stick at anymore. Guys like Clyde McPhatter used to sing their tail ends off! Today I only have a little hope for Texas bands [laughing] . . . Delbert McClinton's still doing some stuff. . . . But melodically and rhythmically, it's not what it was. Take all those imitators of Lou Reed, for example: If they went back and listened to his early stuff, they'd see that he had a whole different feel . . . plus he was a helluva writer. He could really write a lyric. He's been ripped off left, right, and center.

Coming back to Jim Morrison: You know, he felt he had a curse on his head. Because when he was a kid, he was driving with his family near Albuquerque. And there was an Indian on the side of the road, his family stopped, and Morrison went over to the Indian, and this guy— Morrison thought he was some kind of shaman—threw a whammy on him. That's probably when Jim Morrison lost his sense of humor, out there in the desert.

Spells can be effective.

Their power lies in your believing them.

So how do you avoid the so-called "powers" of relentless and overintrusive fans?

Carry a gun! [laughing]

Just don't carry it in your pocket! I can hear people saying: "His plays haven't been the same since."

Thanks for the warning [laughing].

I've noticed that the funniest moments in your plays are often intermixed with a sense of weirdness and sadness.

It's a double-edged thing. If you look at Buster Keaton and Harry Langdon and Stan Laurel, there's something tragic about them. The humor lies in their incredible innocence in the face of life that doesn't make sense.

You've written about the simplicity and purity of Keaton's face and body during the chase scenes of Keaton's films. And I've also noticed that during those climactic scenes, the notions of waking and dreaming, conscious and unconscious, reality and wishes just magically come together—Keaton rushing across a raised drawbridge and a boat just happening to come by to provide him support as he races over it.

Like a true Fool. Things are falling in, everyone's panicking, but he doesn't understand the predicament—it's as if he's in another world. An innocent world.

Laurel and Hardy have a short called *Big Business* in which they cart Christmas trees door-to-door. And one guy whose house they come to doesn't want the tree; he slams the door on them, but the tree's caught, so they ring the bell again . . . and the anger escalates until they're destroying his house, and then he goes outside and destroys their car, while a policeman stands by marking down all the violations, as if he's watching a football game. As they get more and more out of control, the film gets funnier and funnier. It's really funny . . . and tragic.

Like the theatrical masks—one for comedy, one for tragedy. Smiling and weeping.

One on top of the other.

Someone once commented that life is tragic to those who feel and comic to those who think.

I think that to a certain extent that's true. One of the things I look for in actors is a genuine sense of humor. And if they have that, I immediately know that there's a kind of intelligence working there that you won't find in an actor who takes himself so seriously and who's so wrapped up in the Method that he can't see how ridiculous it is. And I much prefer directing the first type of actor rather than someone who's buried in this morose idea of his technique. You have to have a perspective, otherwise you just go under.

As one of the characters in your play Curse of the Starving Class *says: "What's there to envy but an outlook?" One might envy your outlook.*

Well, I've seen people with better ones [laughing] . . . you know, people who never find fault with anybody, for whom everything's great, people who are positive all the time.

Not everyone, I gather, was totally positive about your first playwriting efforts in New York City.

Actually, there was only *one* guy who liked me [laughing]—Michael Smith of *The Village Voice.* Those first reviews were devastating. In fact, I was vulnerable then, and was ready to pack it in and come back to California and get work as a hand on a ranch. But writing has been such a salvation for me for so long that it would be impossible for me to give it up now.

Too late to stop now.

Yeh, it's too late to stop now. . . . Otis Redding. *There* was a great singer!

Has acting also been a salvation?

No, not at all, I don't have the same connection to it. With acting I feel that I'm just struggling to get by. An actor is right on the edge because all he has is the body. . . . Actually, I should say that acting and writing *are* related; I just don't feel the same sense of urgency about acting as I do about writing. I've never been able to write a play while I've been acting in a film. It's difficult to split your participation. You have to be very focused and fully occupied to write . . . you get enraptured for a long time. And it's difficult to do that sitting in an actor's trailer.

And then, of course, you've been directing your recent plays, too. Theoretically, you could actually be someone who directs himself acting in a play that you yourself have written!

Right. And I'm in the process of finishing a screenplay that I'm going to direct, but I'm not going to act in it.

Someone like Woody Allen does it all the time.

He can do it because in his roles he stands outside the character—he comments on the character rather than plays it . . . except in *Broadway Danny Rose,* where he does play a real character. And he's probably the best one around who can write, direct, and act. But I don't think I could direct myself acting, because, for me, the two things are diametrically opposed. I don't see how you can be inside *and* outside at the same time. Acting involves such a deep kind of penetration *in,* and directing demands an observation from the outside.

It's like that line by Bob Dylan: "I punched-myself-in-my-face-with-my-fist."

Well, when you look at the great stand-up comics, that's basically what they're doing—like Lenny Bruce, who was directing himself acting in a play that he'd written.

You yourself have also worked on a lot of film scripts for such directors as Michelangelo Antonioni, Werner Herzog, and Wim Wenders. I heard that one of your early scripts was something called Maxagasm.

Keith Richards had an idea for a film, and I was out at his English country place just after the big drug bust of some of the Stones in the early seventies. It was a weird mansion surrounded by a moat—Keith was in the process of building a moat because he'd just been popped [laughing]. And early every morning I'd wake up and there'd be this huge tractor digging this moat, and I was sort of trapped in the house with a guy who was trying to write the script with me—and I remember that every day a little man would ride up on a bike from the nearby village and deliver some bread to us. Very strange. . . . Needless to say, the script was a disaster, and we never got it off the ground.

I met Keith through an amazing guy named Rufus, who was a member of the Living Theater. I met them both in Rome, actually, when I was working with Antonioni on the script for *Zabriskie Point*. We used to go to a famous discothèque called the Piper Club, where a sort of New Wave, Velvet Underground-type of Italian band used to play. And we would sit around drinking Sambucas with coffee beans in them. And Rufus and Keith would take these little decanterlike glasses, drink them down, and then throw them against the back wall and watch them splatter. We used to do that for about four hours, stumble out of the place, and wander around these piazzas. It was a *lost* time, I'll tell you. . . . But Keith is great. He has the feeling of one of those old Southern guys who just wants to sit around on some back porch and play the blues. He's tougher than nails, and he's got some *hands* on him . . . huge hands.

In Rolling Thunder Logbook *you write about Dylan's "weathered, milky leather hands that tell more than his face about music and where he's been. Ancient, demonic, almost scary, nonhuman hands." And in describing your first meeting with Dylan, you comment that the first thing he said to you was: "We don't have to make any connections" . . . and you didn't know whether he was talking about you and him personally or about the movie you were supposed to be working on with him.*

Bob gets off the hook a lot with that approach [laughing]. He's great, and I love working with him . . . but he would rather not commit than commit [laughing]. I wish you could hear the tune he and I wrote together in the spring of 1985. [The tune, "Brownsville Girl," appears on Dylan's 1986 album *Knocked Out Loaded.*] It was at least twenty minutes long—like a saga!—and it had to do with a guy standing on line and waiting to see an old Gregory Peck movie that he can't quite remember—only pieces of it. And then this whole memory thing happens, unfolding before his very eyes. He starts speaking internally to a woman he'd been hanging out with, recalling their meetings and reliving the whole journey they'd gone on—and then it returns to the guy, who's still standing on line in the rain. The film the song was about was a Gregory Peck Western that Bob had once seen, but he couldn't remember the title. We decided that the title didn't matter, and we spent two days writing the lyrics—Bob had previously composed the melody line, which was already down on tape. He'd already gone through different phases with the song; at one point he talked about making a video out of it. I told him that it should be an opera, that we should extend it—make it an hour and half or so—and perform it like an opera. . . . He's a lot of fun to work with because he's so off-the-wall sometimes. We'd come up with a line and I'd think that we were heading down one trail over here, and then suddenly he'd just throw in this other line, and we'd wind up following it off in some different direction. Sometimes it's frustrating to do that when you're trying to make a wholeness out of something, but it turned out okay.

You've actually done exactly that in many of your plays.

Yeh, but I'm trying to do it less than I used to [laughing].

Writing songs and plays, playing music, acting, directing . . .

It's just been one step at a time. I don't deny that I've had some good luck. My dad had a lot of bad luck. I've had good luck. Luck is a part of it. But I don't know exactly how that works.

When a critic says, "Well, Sam Shepard has now said everything he has to say in A Lie of the Mind, *where can he possibly go from here?" that is, in a way, sort of casting a little doubt-spell, isn't it?*

Yeah, it's trying to do something to you, but you can't pay any attention to that because you've got other things to do. Being surrounded by parasitic people who feed off of your work—well, I guess you've just got to accept it. And I suppose some parasites are okay because they take things off of you.

Once, in New Mexico, I observed these incredibly beautiful red-tailed hawks—with a wing span of five feet—which start out gliding in these arroyos way down low. And these crows come and bother them—they're after fleas and peck at the hawks and drive them nuts because they're looking for something else. And I watched a crow diving at and bothering this one hawk, which just flew higher and higher, until it was so far up that the crow couldn't follow it anymore and had to come back down.

So the answer is to outfly them.

Yeah, outfly them. Avoid situations that are going to take pieces of you. And hide out.

[Los Angeles, 1985]

Bob Dylan

WE WERE DRIVING DOWN SUNSET BOULEVARD—CHRISTMASTIME in L.A. [December 1977]—looking for a place to eat, when Bob Dylan noticed Santa Claus, surrounded by hundreds of stuffed, Day-Glo animals, standing and soliciting on the street. "Santa Claus in the desert," he commented disconcertedly; "it really brings you down."

A few minutes later, we passed a billboard that showed a photo of George Burns pointing to a new album by John Denver and praising it to the skies. "Did you see that movie they appeared in together?" Dylan asked me. "I sort of like George Burns. What was he playing?"

"I saw it on the plane coming out here. He played God," I said.

"That's a helluva role," Dylan replied.

Bob Dylan should know. For years he has been worshiped—and deservedly so. His songs are miracles, his ways mysterious and unfathomable. In words and music, he has reawakened, and thereby altered, our experience of the world. In statement ("He not busy being born is busy dying") and in image ("My dreams are made of iron and steel/With a big bouquet of roses hanging down/From the heavens to the ground") he has kept alive the idea of the poet and artist as *vates*—the visionary eye of the body politic—while keeping himself open to a conception of art that embraces and respects equally Charles Baudelaire and Charley Patton, Arthur Rimbaud and Smokey Robinson.

"Mystery is an essential element in any work of art," says the director Luis Buñuel in a recent *New Yorker* profile by Penelope Gilliatt. "It's usually lacking in film, which should be the most mysterious of all. Most filmmakers are careful not to perturb us by opening the windows of the screen onto their world of poetry. Cinema is a marvelous weapon when it is handled by a free spirit. Of all the means of expression, it is the one that is most like the human imagination. What's the good of it if it apes everything conformist and sentimental in us? It's a curious thing that film can create such moments of compressed ritual. The raising of the everyday to the dramatic."

I happened to read these words during my flight to Los Angeles in December of 1977—having just finished watching the conventional and sentimental in-flight movie—hardly knowing then that, just a day later, I would be seeing a film that perfectly embodied Buñuel's notion of the possibilities of cinema.

Renaldo and Clara—an audacious and remarkable four-hour movie that opened in January 1978—is Bob Dylan's second film. His first, *Eat the Document,* was a kind of antidocumentary, a night journey through the disjointed landscapes of Dylan's and the Band's 1966 world tour, a magic swirling ship of jump cuts, "ready for to fade." It was a fascinating work. But to remain on a given level, no matter how exalted, is a sin, a spiritual teacher once said. And just as it is impossible for Bob Dylan "to sing the same song the same way twice"—as he himself puts it—so his new film is a departure from *Eat the Document,* as it announces the arrival of a visionary cinematic free spirit.

Conceived over a period of ten years, and edited down by Howard Alk and Dylan from 100 hours of footage, *Renaldo and Clara* was shot during the 1975–76 Rolling Thunder Revue, whose participants made up a cast that included Bob Dylan (Renaldo), Sara Dylan (Clara), Joan Baez (the Woman in White), Ronnie Hawkins (Bob Dylan), Ronee Blakely (Mrs. Dylan), Jack Elliott (Longheno de Castro), Bob Neuwirth (the Masked Tortilla), Allen Ginsberg (the Father), David Blue (David Blue), and Roger McGuinn (Roger McGuinn).

WHO ARE YOU, BOB DYLAN? was the headline in the French newspaper read by Jean-Pierre Léaud in Jean-Luc Godard's *Masculin-Féminin.* And the mystery of *Renaldo and Clara* is: "Who is Bob Dylan?" "Who is Renaldo?" and "What is the relationship between them?"

I decided to ask Bob Dylan himself.

"There's Renaldo," he told me, "there's a guy in whiteface singing on the stage, and then there's Ronnie Hawkins playing Bob Dylan. Bob Dylan is listed in the credits as playing Renaldo, yet Ronnie Hawkins is listed as playing Bob Dylan."

"So Bob Dylan," I surmise, "may or may not be in the film."

"Exactly."

"But Bob Dylan made the film."

"Bob Dylan didn't make it. *I* made it."

"I is another," wrote Arthur Rimbaud, and this statement is certainly demonstrated by *Renaldo and Clara,* in which characters in masks and hats—often interchangeable—sit in restaurants and talk, disappear, reappear, exchange flowers, argue, visit cemeteries, play music, travel around in trains and vans and, in one exhilarating scene, dance around

168

at the edge of a beautiful bay, where they join hands and begin singing an American Indian/Hindu Indian-sounding chant to the accompaniment of a *bop-shoo-op-doo-wah-ditty* chorus—a spiritual and rock and roll reunion.

To the anagogic eye, however, the film seems to be about just one man—who could pass for the Jack of Hearts, the leading actor of Dylan's song "Lily, Rosemary, and the Jack of Hearts," a card among cards, an image among images—and just one woman. Together they find themselves in the grip of a series of romantic encounters that are reenactments of the Great Mystery, culminating in the confrontation of the Woman in White (Joan Baez), Clara (Sara Dylan), and Renaldo (Bob Dylan)—a meeting at the border of myth and reality. Using his physical image and name as the raw material of the film, Bob Dylan—like the Renaissance kings of masque and spectacle—moves daringly and ambiguously between fiction, representation, identification, and participation.

Renaldo and Clara, of course, is a film filled with magnificently shot and recorded concert footage of highly charged Dylan performances of songs like "It Ain't Me, Babe," "A Hard Rain's A-Gonna Fall," and "Knockin' on Heaven's Door"—the last of whose delicate and eerie instrumental breaks makes you feel as if you were entering the gates of paradise themselves. Avoiding all of the cinematic clichés of pounding-and-zooming television rock and roll specials, the cameras either subtly choreograph the songs—revealing structures and feelings—or else look at the white-faced Dylan and the accompanying painted musicians in rapturous and intensely held close-ups.

Around these musical episodes Dylan has woven a series of multilayered and multileveled scenes—unconsciously echoing similar movements in films by Jean Cocteau, John Cassavetes, and especially Jacques Rivette—each of which lights up and casts light on all the others. Scenes and characters duplicate and mirror each other, are disassociated and recombined—all of them, in the words of the director, "filled with reason but not with logic." Thus, when Clara (Sara Dylan) says to Renaldo: "I am free . . . I can change," it brings back to us the words spoken earlier on by Renaldo to the Woman in White (Joan Baez): "I haven't changed that much. Have you?" to which the Woman in White replies, "Maybe."

And then there are the correspondences and the doubled worlds. The scenes in the bordello—with Joan Baez and Sara Dylan playing prostitutes and Allen Ginsberg playing a kind of Buddhist john—become an image of something like Vajra Hell—the Tantric Buddhist idea of the unbreakable diamond netherworld. And a musician blocking someone's way backstage becomes the Guardian at the Gates.

What is most adventurous and mysterious about *Renaldo and Clara,* however, is the way it counterpoints music with action, lyrics with dialogue, songs with other songs. In one scene, for example, Rodeo (Sam Shepard) is trying to win over Clara, and on the soundtrack you hear, almost subliminally, what sounds like the chord progressions of "Oh, Sister," but which you later realize is "One Too Many Mornings"—as if the songs themselves were trying to communicate with each other, as if they were saying good-bye to each other:

You're right from your side,
I'm right from mine.
We're both just too many mornings
An' a thousand miles behind.

In another scene, members of the Rolling Thunder Revue join in a reception with members of the Tuscarora Indian tribe, while on the soundtrack we hear Dylan's haunting rehearsal tape version of Curtis Mayfield's "People Get Ready." And, finally, in another scene, Renaldo hurries nervously down a city street—panhandling and making some kind of furtive French connection with the Masked Tortilla (Bob Neuwirth)—to the accompaniment of Dylan's version of "Little Moses," above which we hear powerfully spoken lines from poet Anne Waldman's "Fast Speaking Woman" ("I'm the Druid Woman/I'm the Ibo Woman/I'm the Buddha Woman/I'm the Vibrato Woman").

"Your films make one wonder what's going on in people's minds," says Penelope Gilliatt to Buñuel, to which he responds: "Dreams, and also the most everyday questions: 'What time is it?' 'Do you want to eat?' " And, in spite of the compression and density of most of the scenes in *Renaldo and Clara,* there is also a presentational immediacy and clarity that fixes the scenes in one's mind—like a very special dream one wants to remember.

"I expect this will be a very small film," Buñuel said during the shooting of his recent *That Obscure Object of Desire*—which might, in fact, have served as the title of *Renaldo and Clara.* "One needs just a hole to look out of," Buñuel continued, "like a spider that has spun its web and is remembering what the world outside was like. This hole is the secret of things. An artist can provide an essential margin of alertness."

Renaldo and Clara is a long film—and a much-maligned and neglected film—but it is really an intimate and evanescent one. "Art is the perpetual motion of illusion," says Bob Dylan in the interview that follows—which took place a week before Christmas 1977 in Los Angeles. "The highest purpose of art," Dylan commented, "is to inspire. What else can you do? What else can you do for anyone but inspire them?"

*   *   *

If someone asked me what **Renaldo and Clara** *was about, I'd say: "Art and life, identity and God—with lots of encounters at bars, restaurants, luncheonettes, cabarets, and bus stations."*

Do you want to see it again? Would it be helpful for you to see it again?

You think I'm too confused about the film?

No. I don't think so at all. It isn't just about bus stations and cabarets and stage music and identity—those are elements of it. But it *is* mostly about identity—about everybody's identity. More important, it's about Renaldo's identity, so we superimpose our own vision on Renaldo: it's his vision and it's his dream.

You know what the film is about? It begins with music—you see a guy in a mask [Bob Dylan], you can see through the mask he's wearing, and he's singing "When I Paint My Masterpiece." So right away you know there's an involvement with music. Music is confronting you.

So are lines like: "You can almost think that you're seein' double."

Right. Also on a lyrical level. But you still don't really know . . . and then you're getting off that, and there seems to be a tour. You're hearing things and seeing people . . . it's not *quite* like a tour, but there's some kind of energy like being on a tour. There's a struggle, there's a reporter—who later appears in the restaurant scenes.

All right, then it goes right to David Blue, who's playing pinball and who seems to be the narrator. He's Renaldo's narrator, he's Renaldo's scribe—he belongs to Renaldo.

Yet David Blue talks not about Renaldo but about Bob Dylan and how he, David Blue, first met Dylan in Greenwich Village in the late fifties.

They seem to be the same person after a while. It's something you can only feel but never really know. Any more than you can know whether Willie Sutton pulled all those bank jobs. Any more than you can know who killed Kennedy for sure.

And right away, David Blue says: "Well, what happened was that when I first left my parents' house, I bought *The Myth of Sisyphus.*" Now, that wasn't really the book, but it was pretty close. It was actually *Existentialism and Human Emotions.* So that's it: This film is a post-existentialist movie. We're in the post-existentialist period. What is it? That's what it is.

What could be more existentialist than playing pinball? It's the perfect existentialist game.

It is. I've seen rows and rows of pinball players lined up like ducks. It's a great equalizer.

What about the emotions in Existentialism and Human Emotions?

Human emotions are the great dictator—in this movie as in all movies. . . . I'll tell you what I think of the emotions later. But getting back to David Blue: He's left his home, and right away you're in for something like a triple dimension. Just ten minutes into the movie he says: "I got in the bus. I went down to New York, walked around for four hours, got back on the bus, and went home." And that is exactly what a lot of people are going to feel when they walk into the movie theater: They got on the bus, walked around for four hours, and walked home.

There's another guy, later in the film, who walks out into the night and says to a girl: "This has been a great mistake."

Yeah. You can pick any line in a movie to sum up your feeling about it. But don't forget you don't see that guy anymore after that. . . . He's gone. And that means Renaldo isn't being watched anymore because *he* was watching Renaldo.

Talking about mistakes and seeing double: It's fascinating how easy it is to mistake people in the film for one another. I mistook you, for instance, for the guy driving the carriage (maybe it was you); for Jack Elliott; and I even mistook you for you.

The Masked Tortilla [Bob Neuwirth] is mistaken for Bob Dylan, Bob Dylan is mistaken for Renaldo. And . . . *Bob Dylan is the one with the hat on.* That's who Bob Dylan is—he's the one with the hat on.

172

Almost every man in the film has a hat on.

Right.

All those disguises and masks.

The first mask, as I said, is one you can see through. But they're all masks. In the film, the mask is more important than the face.

All the women in the film seem to turn into one person, too, and a lot of them wear hats. It reminds me of "The Ballad of Frankie Lee and Judas Priest":

> *He just stood there staring*
> *At that big house as bright as any sun,*
> *With four and twenty windows*
> *And a woman's face in ev'ry one.*

This film was made for you [laughing]. Did you see the Woman in White who becomes a different Woman in White? One's mistaken for the other. At first she's only an idea of herself—you see her in the street, later in the carriage. . . . I think the women in the movie are beautiful. They look like they've stepped out of a painting. They're vulnerable, but they're also strong-willed.

"Breaking just like a little girl."

That's the child in everyone. That's the child in everyone that has to be confronted.

"Just Like a Woman" always seemed to me to be somehow about being born: "I can't stay in here . . . I just can't fit." So by confronting the child in you, saying good-bye to childhood, you're born into something bigger. . . . In a way, it's a frightening song.

It always was a frightening song, but that feeling needs to be eliminated.

I was thinking of what looked like a Yiddish cabaret filled with older women listening intently to Allen Ginsberg reading passages from "Kaddish," his great elegy to his mother.

173

Those women are strong in the sense that they know their own identity. It's only the layer of what we're going to reveal in the next film, because women are exploited like anyone else. They're victims just like coal miners.

The poet Robert Bly has written about the image of the Great Mother as a union of four force fields, consisting of the nurturing mother, like Isis (though your Isis seems more ambiguous); the Death Mother (like the woman in "It's All Over Now, Baby Blue"); the Ecstatic Mother (like the girl in "Spanish Harlem Incident"); and the Stone Mother who drives you mad (like Sweet Melinda who leaves you howling at the moon in "Just Like Tom Thumb's Blues"). Traces of these women seem to be in this film as well.

The Death Mother is represented in the film, but I don't know what I should say or can say or shouldn't say about who is who in the movie. I mean, *Who* is the old woman everyone calls Mama—the woman who sings, plays guitar, and reads palms? She reads Allen's palm, saying: "You've been married twice." And me, later on I'm looking at the gravestone marked HUSBAND, and Ginsberg asks: "Is that going to happen to you?" And I say: "I want an unmarked grave." But of course I'm saying this as Renaldo.

In Tarantula *you wrote your own epitaph:*

Here lies bob dylan
killed by a discarded Oedipus
who turned
around
to investigate a ghost
and discovered that
the ghost too was more than one person.

Yeah, way back then I was thinking of this film. I've had this picture in mind for a long time—years and years. Too many years. . . . Renaldo is oppressed. He's oppressed because he's born. We don't really know who Renaldo is. We just know what he isn't. He isn't the Masked Tortilla. Renaldo is the one with the hat, but he's not wearing a hat. I'll tell you what this movie is: It's like life exactly, but not an imitation of it. It transcends life, and it's not like life.

That paradox is toppling me over.

I'll tell you what my film is about: It's about naked alienation of the inner self against the outer self—alienation taken to the extreme. And it's about integrity. My next film is about obsession. The hero is an arsonist . . . but he's not really a hero.

Renaldo and Clara seems to me to be about obsession, too.

That's true, but only in the way it applies to integrity.

The idea of integrity comes across in a lot of your songs and in lines like: "To live outside the law, you must be honest" and "She doesn't have to say she's faithful,/Yet she's true, like ice, like fire."

We talked about emotions before. You can't be a slave to your emotions. If you're a slave to your emotions you're dependent on your emotions, and you're only dealing with your conscious mind. But the film is about the fact that you have to be faithful to your subconscious, unconscious, superconscious—as well as to your conscious. Integrity is a facet of honesty. It has to do with knowing yourself.

At the end of the film, Renaldo is with two women in a room (the Woman in White played by Joan Baez and Clara played by Sara Dylan), and he says: "Evasiveness is only in the mind—truth is on many levels. . . . Ask me anything and I'll tell you the truth." Clara and the Woman in White both ask him: "Do you love her?" as they point to each other—not: "Do you love me?"

Possessiveness. It was a self-focused kind of question. And earlier, one of the women in the whorehouse talks about the ego-protection cords she wears around her neck. Do you remember that? . . . In the scene you mentioned, did you notice that Renaldo was looking at the newspaper which had an article on Bob Dylan and Joan Baez in it? Joan Baez and Bob Dylan at this point are an illusion. It wasn't planned that way. Joan Baez without Bob Dylan isn't too much of an illusion because she's an independent woman and her independence asserts itself. But Joan Baez with Bob Dylan *is*.

So at the moment you open up that newspaper, art and life really come together.

Exactly

And what about the moment when Joan Baez, looking at Clara, says: "Who is this woman?" and you cut to your singing "Sara"? Talk about art and life!

It's as far as you can take it—meaning personally and generally. Who is this woman? Obviously, this woman is a figment of the material world. Who is this woman who has no name? Who is this woman, she says . . . who is this woman, as if she's talking about herself. Who this woman is is told to you, earlier on, when you see her coming out of the church carrying a rope. You know she means business, you know she has a purpose.

Another way of putting it is: The singer's character onstage is always becoming Renaldo. By singing "Sara," the singer comes as close to Renaldo as he can get. It brings everything as close as possible without two becoming one.

It was pretty amazing to see you use your personal life and the myth of your life so nakedly in that scene with Renaldo and the two women.

Right, but you're talking to me as a director now.

Still, you do have that scene with Joan Baez and Sara Dylan.

Well, Sara Dylan here is working as Sara Dylan. She has the same last name as Bob Dylan, but we may not be related. If she couldn't have played the role of Clara, she wouldn't have done it.

Is she talking about her real problems or pretending that she's an adventurer?

We can make anybody's problems our problems.

Some people will obviously think that this film either broke up your marriage or is a kind of incantation to make your marriage come back together.

Either one of those statements I can't relate to. It has nothing to do with the breakup of my marriage. My marriage is over. I'm divorced. This film is a film.

Why did you make yourself so vulnerable?

You must be vulnerable to be sensitive to reality. And to me being vulnerable is just another way of saying that one has nothing more to lose. I don't have anything but darkness to lose. I'm way beyond that. The worst thing that could happen is that the film will be accepted and that the next one will be compared unfavorably to this one.

Strangely, the scene where the two women confront Renaldo reminds me of King Lear, *in which each of the daughters has to say how much she loves her father.*

You're right. Renaldo sees himself as Cordelia.

I've always interpreted some of The Basement Tapes *as being concerned with ideas from* King Lear: *"Too much of nothing/Can make a man abuse a king"; "Oh what dear daughter 'neath the sun/Would treat a father so,/To wait upon him hand and foot/And always tell him, 'No'?"*

Exactly. In the later years it changed from "king" to "clown."

King Lear had a fool around him, too, and when the fool leaves, Cordelia comes back. She takes his place, and he takes hers.

The roles are all interchangeable.

As in "Tangled Up in Blue" and as in your movie.

Yes it is.

Were you specifically influenced by King Lear *when you wrote songs like "Tears of Rage"?*

No. Songs like that were based on the concept that one is one.

". . . and all alone and ever more shall be so."

Exactly. What comes is gone forever every time.

But one is difficult to deal with, so Christians gave us the Trinity.

177

The Christians didn't bring in anything—it was the Greeks.

Jesus is a very strong figure in Renaldo and Clara. *There's that song by you called "What Will You Do When Jesus Comes?" There's the woman who says to you in the restaurant: "There's nowhere to go. Just stand and place yourself like the cross and I'll receive you." And then there are the shots of the huge cement crucifix in the Catholic Grotto.*

Right. Jesus is the most identifiable figure in Western culture, and yet he was exploited, used, and exploited. We all have been.

There's also that scene, near the end of the film, where Allen Ginsberg takes you around to see the glassed-in sculptures of the Stations of the Cross—and we see Jesus killed for the second time and then buried under the weight of the cross. On one level, the film is about the Stations of the Cross, isn't it?

Yeah, you're right, like the double vision having to be killed twice. Like why does Jesus really die?

Spiritually or politically?

Realistically. . . . Because he's a healer. Jesus is a healer. So he goes to India, finds out how to be a healer, and becomes one. But see, I believe that he overstepped his duties a little bit. He accepted and took on the bad karma of all the people he healed. And he was filled with so much bad karma that the only way out was to burn him up.

In my film, we're looking at masks a lot of the time. And then when the dream becomes so solidified that it has to be taken to the stage of reality, then you'll see stone, you'll see a statue—which is even a further extension of the mask: the statue of Mary in front of the statue of Jesus-on-the-cross in the Crucifix Grotto.

Throughout the film, I also noticed the continual reappearance of the red rose. Every woman has a rose.

It has a great deal to do with what's happening in the movie. Do you remember the woman in the carriage? She's bringing a rose to Renaldo, who gives it back to her.

But then it appears in your hat when you're singing.

By that time it's all fallen apart and shattered, the dream is gone . . . it could be anywhere after that.

Joan Baez carries one when she's with Mama. And then the violinist Scarlet Rivera gives it to you in your dressing room.

That's right. The rose is a symbol of fertility.

Also of the soul. The Romance of the Rose—*the dreamer's vision of the soul.*

That's right. . . . The most mysterious figure in the film is the conductor on the train. Do you remember him?

He's the guy who tells the Masked Tortilla—who says he's going to a wedding—that he's only been on the train for four hours (there's that magical four hours again!) and not for the six days that he imagines.

Yeah, he tells him, too, that he's going to possibly the largest city in the East.

I figured it was New York.

No. The largest city in the *East!*

The Magi!

That's not exactly what he's talking about—it's more like the holy crossroads.

There's another scene like that in which Mick Ronson is blocking Ronnie Hawkins's way to a backstage area. He seemed like some kind of guardian.

He's the Guardian of the Gates. But scenes like these work in terms of feeling. It's like with Tarot cards—you don't have to be confused as to what they mean . . . someone else who knows can read them for you.

"Nothing is revealed," you sing at the end of "The Ballad of Frankie Lee and Judas Priest." Is anything revealed at the end of Renaldo and Clara?

Yeah, I'll tell you what the film reveals. This film reveals that there's a whole lot to reveal beneath the surface of the soul, but it's unthinkable. . . . That's exactly what it reveals. It reveals the depths that there are to reveal. And that's the most you can ask, because things are really very invisible. You can't reveal the invisible. And this film goes as far as we can to reveal that.

Under a statue of Isis in the city of Saïs is the following inscription: "I am everything that was, that is, that shall be. . . . Nor has any mortal ever been able to discover what lies under my veil."

That's a fantastic quotation. That's true, exactly. Once you see what's under the veil, what happens to you? You die, don't you, or go blind?

I wanted to tie in two things we've talked about: the idea of integrity and the idea of Jesus. In your song "I Want You," you have the lines:
  Now all my fathers, they've gone down,
  True love they've been without it.
  But all their daughters put me down
  'Cause I don't think about it.
These are some of my favorite lines of yours, and to me they suggest that real desire is stronger than frustration or guilt.

I know. It's incredible you find that there. I know it's true. And in *Renaldo and Clara* there's no guilt. But that's why people will take offense at it, if they are offended by it in any way, because of the lack of guilt in the movie. None at all.

This brings us back to Jesus.

Jesus is . . . well, I'm not using Jesus in the film so much as I'm using the *concept* of Jesus—the idea of Jesus as a man, not the virgin birth.

But what about the concept of masochism associated with Jesus?

That's what happened to Jesus. People relate to the masochism, to the spikes in his hand, to the blood coming out, to the fact that he was crucified. What would have happened to him if he hadn't been crucified? That's what draws people to him. There are only signals of that in this film—like a fingernail blade at one point.

What about the line in "Wedding Song": "Your love cuts like a knife."

Well, it's bloodletting, it's what heals all disease. Neither aggression nor anger interests me. Violence only does on an interpretive level, only when it's a product of reason.

People are attracted to blood. I'm personally not consumed by the desire to drink the blood. But bloodletting is meaningful in that it can cure disease. But we didn't try to make a film of that nature. This film concerns itself with the dream. There's no blood in the dream, the dream is cold. This film concerns itself with the depth of the dream—the dream as seen in the mirror.

The next film might have some blood. . . . I'm trying to locate Lois Smith to be in it. She would represent the idea of innocence. Do you know who she is? She was the barmaid in *East of Eden*. I'm trying to line up some people for the film, and I can't find her. . . .

For some reason I've just thought of my favorite singer.

Who is that?

Om Kalsoum—the Egyptian woman who died a few years ago. She was my favorite.

What did you like about her?

It was her heart.

Do you like dervish and Sufi singing, by the way?

Yeah, that's where my singing really comes from . . . except that I sing in America. I've heard too much Leadbelly, really, to be too much influenced by the whirling dervishes.

Now that we somehow got onto this subject, what musicians do you like at the moment? New Wave groups?

No. I'm not interested in them. I think Alice Cooper is an overlooked songwriter. I like Ry Cooder. And I like Dave Mason's version of something which is on the jukebox right now.

I wonder what you think of the guy who ends your movie singing that fulsome, crooning version of "In the Morning" with those memorable lines: "I'll be yawning into the morning of my life." Why is he there?

The film had to end with him because he represents the fact that Renaldo could be dreaming. And he might be singing for Renaldo—representing him, the darkness representing the light.

He's like what's happened to one sentimental part of rock and roll in the seventies.

He's not rock and roll.

Rock and roll isn't rock and roll anymore.

You're right, there's no more rock and roll. It's an imitation, we can forget about that. Rock and roll has turned itself inside out. I never did do rock and roll. I'm just doing the same old thing I've always done.

You've never sung a rock and roll song?

No, I never have. Only in spirit.

You can't really dance to one of your songs.

I couldn't.

Imagine dancing to "Rainy Day Woman #12 & 35." It's kind of alienating. Everyone thought it was about being stoned, but I always thought it was about being alone.

So did I. You could write about that for years. . . . Rock and roll ended with Phil Spector. The Beatles weren't rock and roll either. Nor the Rolling Stones. Rock and roll ended with Little Anthony and the Imperials. Pure rock and roll.

With "Goin' Out of My Head"?

The one before that. . . . Rock and roll ended in 1959.

When did it begin for you?

1954.

What is there now?

182

Programmed music. Quadruple tracking.

What do you think about the seventies?

The seventies I see as a period of reconstruction after the sixties, that's all. That's why people say: "Well, it's boring, nothing's really happening," and that's because wounds are healing. By the eighties, anyone who's going to be doing anything will have his or her cards showing. You won't be able to get back in the game in the eighties.

I came across something you wrote a while back:

> *Desire . . . never fearful*
> *finally faithful*
> *it will guide me well*
> *across all bridges*
> *inside all tunnels*
> *never failin'.*

I even remember where I wrote that. I wrote that in New Hampshire. I think I was all alone.

Here's something else you wrote:

> *Mine shall be a strong loneliness*
> *dissolvin' deep*
> *t' the depths of my freedom*
> *an' that, then, shall*
> *remain my song.*

You seem to have stayed true to that feeling.

I haven't had any reason to stray.

In "The Times They Are A-Changin' " you sing: "He that gets hurt/ Will be he who has stalled." What has kept you unstalled?

I don't know. Mainly because I don't believe in this life.

The Buddhist tradition talks about illusion, the Jewish tradition about allusion. Which do you feel closer to?

I believe in both, but I probably lean to allusion. I'm not a Buddhist. I believe in life, but not this life.

What life do you believe in?

Real life.

Do you ever experience real life?

I experience it all the time, it's beyond this life.

I wanted to read to you two Hasidic texts that somehow remind me of your work. The first says that in the service of God, one can learn three things from a child and seven from a thief. "From a child you can learn: 1) always to be happy; 2) never to sit idle; and 3) to cry for everything one wants. From a thief you should learn: 1) to work at night; 2) if one cannot gain what one wants in one night, to try again the next night; 3) to love one's co-workers just as thieves love each other; 4) to be willing to risk one's life even for a little thing; 5) not to attach too much value to things even though one has risked one's life for them—just as a thief will resell a stolen article for a fraction of its real value; 6) to withstand all kinds of beatings and tortures but to remain what you are; and 7) to believe that your work is worthwhile and not be willing to change it."

Who wrote that?

A Hasidic rabbi.

Which one?

Dov Baer, the Maggid of Mezeritch.

That's the most mind-blazing chronicle of human behavior I think I've ever heard. . . . How can I get a copy of that? I'll put it on my wall. There's a man I would follow. That's a real hero. A real hero.

Another Hasidic rabbi once said that you can learn something from everything. Even from a train, a telephone, and a telegram. From a train, he said, you can learn that in one second one can miss everything. From a telephone you can learn that what you say over here can be heard over there. And from a telegram that all words are counted and charged.

It's a cosmic statement. Where do you get all of these rabbis' sayings? Those guys are really wise. I tell you, I've heard gurus and yogis and philosophers and politicians and doctors and lawyers, teachers of all kinds . . . and these rabbis really had something going.

They're like Sufis, but they speak and teach with more emotion.

As I said before, I don't believe in emotion. They use their hearts, their hearts don't use them.

In one second missing everything on a train . . . do you think that means that you can miss the train or miss seeing something from the train window?

That's a statement of revelation. I think it means that in one moment you can miss everything because you're not there. You just watch it, and you know you're missing it.

What about the telephone—what you say here is heard over there?

That means you're never that far away from the ultimate God.

And words being counted and charged.

That's very truthful, too. That everything you say and think is all being added up.

How are you coming out?

You know, I'll tell you: lately I've been catching myself. I've been in some scenes, and I say: "Holy shit, I'm not here alone." I've never had that experience before the past few months. I've felt this strange, eerie feeling that I wasn't all alone, and I'd better know it.

Do you watch what you say?

I always try to watch what I say because I try not to say anything I don't mean.

Maybe Renaldo has that problem at the end of your movie?

No, Renaldo's on top of it, he's on top of circumstance. He's not going to say too much 'cause he knows he doesn't know much. Now me, obviously I'm talking and saying things, and I *will* talk and say things, but that's because I think I'm going to mean them . . . or I feel I *mean* them now. I'm not just talking to hear myself. But Renaldo is *not* saying anything just because he knows that *what* he says is being heard and that therefore he doesn't know what to say. No, he says some very incredible and important things when he's confronted with his *allusion.* You know, he does say: "Do I love you like I love her? No." "Do I love her like I love you? No." He can't say any more than that . . . you don't have to know any more about him than that. That's all you have to know about him, that's all you have to know about Bob Dylan.

At that moment in the film, you cut into a performance of your song "Catfish"—"Nobody can throw the ball like Catfish can." It's almost jokey after that intense preceding scene.

It's treated more in the way of music, getting back to the idea that music is truthful. And music *is* truthful. Everything's okay, you put on a record, someone's playing an instrument—that changes the vibe. Music attracts the angels in the universe. A group of angels sitting at a table are going to be attracted by that.

So we always get back to the music in the film. We made a point of doing it, as if we had to do it. You're not going to see music in the movies as you do in this film. We don't have any filler. You don't see any doors close or any reverse shots which are just there to take up time until you get to the next one. We didn't want to take time away from other shots.

A lot of hold shots, not enough of them. When the woman is walking down the street with a rope, that's a hold shot. David Blue is on a hold shot for six minutes the first time you see him.

I know this film is too long. It may be four hours too long—I don't care. To me, it's not long enough. I'm not concerned how long something is. I want to see a set shot. I *feel* a set shot. I don't feel all this motion and boom-boom. We can fast cut when we want, but the power comes in the ability to have faith that it is a meaningful shot.

You know who understood this? Andy Warhol. Warhol did a lot for American cinema. He was before his time. But Warhol and Hitchcock and Peckinpah and Tod Browning . . . they were important to me. I figured Godard had the accessibility to make what he made, he broke new ground. I never saw any film like *Breathless*, but once you saw it, you said: "Yeah, man, why didn't I do that, I could have done that." Okay, he did it, but he couldn't have done it in America.

But what about a film like Sam Fuller's Forty Guns *or Joseph Lewis's* Gun Crazy?

Yeah, I just heard Fuller's name the other day. I think American film-makers are the best. But I also like Kurosawa, and my favorite director is Buñuel; it doesn't surprise me that he'd say those amazing things you quoted to me before from *The New Yorker*.

I don't know what to tell you. In one way I don't consider myself a filmmaker at all. In another way I do. To me, *Renaldo and Clara* is my first real film. I don't know who will like it. I made it for a specific bunch of people and myself, and that's all. That's how I wrote "Blowin' in the Wind" and "The Times They Are A-Changin' "—they were written for a certain crowd of people and for certain artists, too. Who knew they were going to be big songs?

The film, in a way, is a culmination of a lot of your ideas and obsessions.

That may be true, but I hope it also has meaning for other people who aren't that familiar with my songs, and that other people can see themselves in it, because I don't feel so isolated from what's going on. There are a lot of people who'll look at the film without knowing who anybody is in it. And they'll see it more purely.

Eisenstein talked of montage in terms of attraction—shots attracting other shots—then in terms of shock, and finally in terms of fusion and synthesis, and of overtones. You seem to be really aware of the overtones in your film, if you know what I mean?

I sure do.

Eisenstein once wrote: "The Moscow Art Theater is my deadly enemy. It is the exact antithesis of all I am trying to do. They string their emotions together to give a continuous illusion of reality. I take photographs of reality and then cut them up so as to produce emotions."

What we did was to cut up reality and make it more real   Every one from the cameramen to the water boy, from the wardrobe people to the sound people, was just as important as anyone else in the making of the film. There weren't any roles that well-defined. The money was coming in the front door and going out the back door; the Rolling Thunder tour sponsored the movie. And I had faith and trust in the people who helped me do the film, and they had faith and trust in me.

In the movie, there's a man behind a luncheonette counter who talks a lot about truth—he's almost like the Greek chorus of the film.

Yeah, we often sat around and talked about that guy. He *is* the chorus.

That guy at one point talks about the Movement going astray and about how everyone got bought off. How come you didn't sell out and just make a commercial film?

I don't have any cinematic vision to sell out. It's all for me so I can't sell out. I'm not working for anybody. What was there to sell out?

Well, a movie like Welcome to L.A. *is a kind of moralistic exploitation film—and many people nowadays think that it's a significant statement. You could have sold out to the vision of the times.*

Right. I have my point of view and my vision, and nothing tampers with it because it's all that I've got. I don't have anything to sell out.

Renaldo and Clara *has certain similarities to the recent films of Jacques Rivette. Do you know his work?*

I don't. But I wish they'd do it in this country, I'd feel a lot safer. I mean I wouldn't get so much resistance and hostility. I can't believe that people think that four hours is too long for a film. As if people had so much to do. You can see an hour-long movie that seems like ten hours. I think the vision is strong enough to cut through all of that. But we may be kicked right out of Hollywood after this film is released and have to go to Bolivia. In India, they show twelve-hour movies. Americans are spoiled, they expect art to be like wallpaper with no effort, just to be there.

I should have asked you this before, but how much of the film is improvised and how much determined beforehand?

About a third is improvised, about a third is determined, and about a third is blind luck.

What about, for instance, the scene in which Ronnie Hawkins tries to get a farm girl to go on tour with him, trying to convince her by saying something like: "God's not just in the country, God's in the city, too . . . God's everywhere, so let's seize the day."

In that scene, Ronnie was given five subjects to hit on. He could say anything he wanted as long as he covered five points. Obviously, God was a subject relevant to the movie. Then he talked about the Father. Now get this: In the film there's the character of the Father played by Allen Ginsberg. But in Ronnie's scene, the farmer's daughter talks about *her* father. That's the same father.

Another half-improvised scene is the one in which Ramone—the dead lover of Mrs. Dylan [played by Ronee Blakeey]—appears as a ghost in the bathroom, and they argue in front of the mirror.

How does the audience know that that's "Mrs. Dylan"?

She's so identified later on in the film. It's just like Hitchcock. Hitchcock would lay something down, and an hour later you'd figure it out—but if you want to know, you wait and find out. It's not given to you on a platter.

Hitchcock puts himself into each of his films—once. You put yourself in hundreds of places and times!

Right [laughing]. I've tried to learn a lack of fear from Hitchcock.

Did the John Cassavetes movies influence you at all in scenes such as the one in the bathroom?

No, not at all. But I think it all comes from the same place. I'm probably interested in the same things Cassavetes is interested in.

189

What are those?

Timing, for example, and the struggle to break down complexity into simplicity.

Timing of relationships?

The relationships of human reason. It's all a matter of timing. The movie creates and holds the time. That's what it should do—it should hold that time, breathe in that time, and stop time in doing that. It's like if you look at a painting by Cézanne, you get lost in that painting for that period of time. And you breathe—yet time is going by and you wouldn't know it, you're spellbound.

In Cézanne, things that you might take as being decoration actually turn out to be substantial.

That's exactly what happens in *Renaldo and Clara.* Things which appear merely decorative usually, later on, become substantial. It just takes a certain amount of experience with the film to catch on to that. For example, Allen Ginsberg. You first hear his name, just his name. . . .

And then you get a glimpse of him at that weird, monomaniacal poetry reading.

It's not as weird as it should be. Weirdness is exactness.

One quick question about Hurricane Carter, whom you show in the film. Do you think that he was guilty?

I don't personally think he is. I put that sequence in the film because he's a man who's not unlike anyone else in the film. He's a righteous man, a very philosophic man—he's not your typical bank robber or mercy slayer. He deserves better than what he got.

You told me that you plan to make twelve more films, but I gather you're not giving up on songwriting and touring.

I have to get back to playing music because unless I do, I don't really feel alive. I don't feel I can be a filmmaker all the time. I have to play in front of the people in order just to keep going.

In "Wedding Song" you sing: "I love you more than ever/Now that the past is gone." But in "Tangled Up in Blue" you sing: "But all the while I was alone/The past was close behind." Between these two couplets lies an important boundary.

We allow our past to exist. Our credibility is based on our past. But deep in our soul we have no past. I don't think we have a past, any more than we have a name. You can say we have a past if we have a future. Do we have a future? No. So how can our past exist if the future doesn't exist?

So what are the songs on Blood on the Tracks *about?*

The present.

Why did you say, "I love you more than ever/Now that the past is gone"?

That's delusion. That's gone.

And what about "And all the while I was alone/The past was close behind"?

That's more delusion. Delusion is close behind.

When your "Greek chorus" restaurant owner talks about the Movement selling itself out, you next cut to you singing "Tangled Up in Blue," which is, in part, about what has happened in and to the past.

But we're only dealing with the past in terms of being able to be healed by it. We can communicate only because we both agree that this is a glass and this is a bowl and that's a candle and there's a window here and there are lights out in the city. Now I might not agree with that. Turn this glass around and it's something else. Now I'm hiding it in a napkin. Watch it now. Now you don't even know it's there. It's the past. . . . I don't even deal with it. I don't think seriously about the past, the present, or the future. I've spent enough time thinking about these things and have gotten nowhere.

But didn't you when you wrote Blood on the Tracks? *Why is it so intense?*

Because there's physical blood in the soul, and flesh and blood are portraying it to you. Willpower. Willpower is what makes it an intense album . . . but certainly not anything to do with the past or the future. Willpower is telling you that we are agreeing on what is what.

What about "Idiot Wind"?

Willpower.

Why have you been able to keep so in touch with your anger throughout the years, as revealed in songs like "Can You Please Crawl Out Your Window?" and "Positively 4th Street"?

Willpower. With strength of will you can do anything. With willpower you can determine your destiny.

Can you really know where your destiny is leading you?

Yeah, when you're on top of your game. . . . Anger and sentimentality go right next to each other, and they're both superficial. Chagall made a lot of sentimental paintings. And Voltaire wrote a lot of angry books.

What is "Idiot Wind"?

It's a little bit of both because it uses all the textures of strict philosophy, but basically it's a shattered philosophy that doesn't have a title, and it's driven across with willpower. Willpower is what you're responding to.

In your film you show a bearded poet in Hasidic garb who speaks in an Irish brogue and carries a gun. He tells us that he doesn't care about being fast but about being accurate. Is that how you feel now?

Yeah. Everyone admires the poet, no matter if he's a lumberjack or a football player or a car thief. If he's a poet, he'll be admired and respected.

You used to say you were a trapeze artist.

Well, I see the poet in every man and woman.

192

Rimbaud's grave doesn't even mention the fact that he was a poet, but rather that he was an adventurer.

Exactly. But I don't try to adopt or imitate Rimbaud in my work. I'm not interested in imitation.

I've always associated you with Rimbaud. Illuminations and Fireworks. Do you believe in reincarnation?

I believe in this—if you want to take reincarnation as a subject: Let's say a child is conceived inside of a woman's belly, and was planted there by a man. Nine months before that seed is planted, there's nothing. Ten, twelve, thirteen months . . . two years before that seed is planted, maybe there's the germination of that seed. That comes from food intake into the bloodstream. Food can be a side of beef or a carrot on a shelf. But that's what makes it happen.

In another lifetime—you're in a supermarket and there's a package of carrots right there . . . *that* possibly could be *you. That* kind of reincarnation. . . . And how did that carrot get there? It got there through the ground. It grew through the ground with the help of a piece of animal shit. It has to do with the creation and destruction of *time.* Which means it's immense. Five million years is nothing—it's a drop in a bucket. I don't think there's enough *time* for reincarnation. It would take thousands or millions of years and light miles for any real kind of reincarnation.

I think one can be conscious of different vibrations in the universe, and these can be picked up. But reincarnation from the twelfth to the twentieth century—I say it's impossible.

So you take reincarnation on a cellular level, and when I say "Rimbaud and you," you take it as an affinity.

Maybe my spirit passed through the same places as his did. We're all wind and dust anyway, and we could have passed through many barriers at different times.

What about your line: "Sweet Goddess/Born of a blinding light and a changing wind" in the song "Tough Mama"?

That's the mother and father, the yin and yang. That's the coming together of destiny and the fulfillment of destiny.

193

George Harrison once said that your lines:

> Look out kid
> It's somethin' you did
> God knows when
> But you're doin' it again

from "Subterranean Homesick Blues" seemed to be a wonderful description of karma.

Karma's not reincarnation. There's no proof of reincarnation and there's no proof of karma, but there's a *feeling* of karma. We don't even have any proof that the universe exists. We don't have any proof that we are even sitting here. We can't prove that we're really alive. How can we prove we're alive by other people saying we're alive?

All I have to do is kick a rock.

Yeah, you're saying *you're* alive, but the rock isn't going to tell you. The rock don't feel it.

If you take reality to be unreal, then you make unreality real. What's real to you? Art?

Art is the perpetual motion of illusion. The highest purpose of art is to inspire. What else can you do? What else can you do for anyone but inspire them?

What are your new songs like?

My new songs are new for me, and they accomplish what I wanted to accomplish when I started thinking about them. Very seldom do you finish something and then abandon it, and very seldom do you abandon something with the attitude that you've gotten what you started out to get. Usually you think, "Well, it's too big," you get wasted along the way someplace, and it just trails off . . . and what you've got is what you've got and you just do the best with it. But very seldom do you ever come out with what you put in. And I think I've done that now for the first time since I was writing two songs a day way back when. My experience with film helped me in writing the songs. I probably wouldn't have written any more songs if I hadn't made this film. I would have been bummed out, I wouldn't have been able to do what I knew could be done.

I know I'm being nostalgic, but I loved hearing you sing "Little Moses" in Renaldo and Clara.

I used to play that song when I performed at Gerdes Folk City. It's an old Carter Family song, and it goes something like:

Away by the waters so wide
The ladies were winding their way,
When Pharoah's little daughter
Stepped down in the water
To bathe in the cool of the day.
And before it got dark,
She opened the ark,
And saw the sweet infant so gay.

Then little Moses grows up, slays the Egyptian, leads the Jews—it's a great song. And I thought it fit pretty well into the movie.

Everybody's in this film: the Carter Family, Hank Williams, Woody Guthrie, Beethoven. Who is going to understand this film? Where are the people to understand this film—a film which needs no understanding?

Who understands "Sad-Eyed Lady of the Lowlands"?

I do. . . . It's strange. I finally feel in the position of someone whom people want to interview enough that they'll fly you into town, put you up in a hotel, pay all your expenses, and give you a tour of the city. I'm finally in that position.

I once went to see the King of the Gypsies in Southern France. This guy had twelve wives and a hundred children. He was in the antique business and had a junkyard, but he'd had a heart attack before I'd come to see him. All his wives and children had left. And the gypsy clan had left him with only one wife and a couple of kids and a dog. What happens is that after he dies they'll all come back. They smell death and they leave. That's what happens in life. And I was very affected by seeing that.

Did you feel something like that in the past five years?

You're talking about 1973? I don't even remember 1973, I'm talking about the spring of 1975. There was a lack of targets at that time. But I don't remember what happened last week.

But you probably remember your childhood clearly.

My childhood is so far away . . . it's like I don't even remember being a child. I think it was someone else who was a child. Did you ever think like that? I'm not sure that what happened to me yesterday was true.

But you seem sure of yourself.

I'm sure of my dream self, I live in my dreams, I don't really live in the actual world.

*   *   *

    "I'll let you be in my dreams
      if I can be in yours.
      I said that."
               BOB DYLAN: 1963

[Los Angeles, 1977]

Lawrence Kushner

JUST ABOUT FORTY CENTURIES AGO, THE NINETY-NINE-YEAR-OLD patriarch Abraham (so the Bible tells us) came to the end of his travels and settled in the plain of Mamre (which is in present-day Hebron). Having smashed his father's idols, this Chaldean trader, clan leader, warrior-priest, and visionary monotheist had, at God's command, set out twenty-four years earlier from Ur and Haran; had journeyed more than two thousand miles; and had finally entered Canaan. Here, in Shechem, the patriarch built his first altar to the One God. (It was here, too, that his grandson Jacob would rest his head on a stone, fall asleep, and dream of angels ascending and descending the rungs of a ladder that reached from the earth up to heaven.) But famine drove Abraham and his retinue down to Egypt; though when he returned, he came back once again to Shechem and, finally, to Hebron.

Now, God had spoken to Abraham and said: "I will bestow My blessing upon you and make your descendants as numerous as the stars of heaven and the sands on the seashore." God promised Abraham that His covenant would be established with a son by Sarah, who was now ninety years old. And still they had no child.

Then, one afternoon in Hebron—so the Bible tells us—Abraham was sitting at the entrance to his tent. "And the Lord appeared to him by the oaks of Mamre . . . in the heat of the day." Abraham raised his eyes. "And behold, three people were standing by him; and he looked and he ran to meet them from the entrance of the tent; and he bowed to the ground. And he said, 'My Lords, if I have found favor in your eyes do not pass on by your servant. Let now a little water be brought and wash your feet and recline under the tree. I will get a little food and you will refresh yourselves, afterwards you will travel on, since you have come by your servant's way.' They said, 'Do as you have said.' And Abraham hurried to the tent, to Sarah, and he said, 'Hurry, three measures of fine flour; knead and make cakes.' And Abraham ran to the herd and he took a calf.''

These three messengers (angels) had come to inform the then one-hundred-year-old patriarch and an incredulous, laughing Sarah ("After I am waxed old shall I have pleasure, my lord being old also?") that they would have a son named Isaac, "for nothing was too hard for the Lord." And nothing was. (And Isaac was born.) But before the three messengers could make their astonishing announcement, etiquette required that lunch be prepared and served. So Abraham "ran to the herd" and "took a calf."

Now, in between the *running* and the *taking,* certain Jewish midrashic texts have speculated that the calf that Abraham was chasing ran away and entered a cave (the Cave of Machpelah). And according to these texts, Abraham followed the calf . . . when suddenly, he saw a shining light—a river of light. And as he moved toward the beam, the earth lifted, revealing nothing less than the graves of Adam and Eve in the Garden of Eden: Light shone above them, the air was filled with a sweet fragrance, and the image of Adam rose and smiled at Abraham, who now knew that this was the place meant for his own burial.*

In his book entitled *The River of Light: Spirituality, Judaism, and the Evolution of Consciousness,* Rabbi Lawrence Kushner enters into and explores Abraham's astonishing near-death vision, much as the patriarch himself entered into and experienced the mysteries of the cave, "slipping through the 'scriptural text' of his daily life," as Kushner writes, "into the primordial light of consciousness itself. Into that river of light that nourishes all being."

"Scripture," Lawrence Kushner goes on to explain, "says only that Abraham went to the herd, got a calf, and returned. It does not say or even suggest that he chased one into a cave, discovered Adam and Eve, and found the Garden of Eden. In no way can it be inferred from the narrative. This deliberative leaving of the text—and returning to the next word—is called, in Hebrew, *Midrash.* Not the creation of a story from out of thin air, which is called 'fantasy.' Nor the elaboration of one word or event and returning to this same word or event, which is called 'commentary.' But the deliberate filling in of the gap between two words. Not to dissolve their individuality, but to fuse them into the

---

* Eventually, according to the Bible, Abraham would buy the Cave of Machpelah from its owner, Ephron the Hittite, for 400 shekels of silver. And inside the still-standing limestone-colored walls, built 2,100 years ago by King Herod, one can today pay a visit to the sepulchral monuments—covered with embroidered canopies—over which are hidden the caves where Abraham and Sarah, Isaac and Rebecca, and Jacob and Leah are supposed to be buried.

even greater totality from which they have risen and of which they are only a part. This is called Midrash."

Midrash (which derives from the Hebrew root "to search out") is, first of all, a voyage of discovering and uncovering meanings in sacred texts that mystics believe are *already* present in them. (As it has been said about the Torah: "Turn it and turn it again, for everything is contained therein.") But for Lawrence Kushner, holy texts are also like Great Dreams; and he writes, "If Scripture is like a dream, then Midrash is like therapy. . . . Midrash, like therapy, does not seek to change the text. Rather, by joining its fragments together in a new and more coherent pattern of meaning, it seeks to set it free of old, paralyzing stereotypes. We open our eyes to the words/personality before us and see it as a new creation. As if it were born just this moment."

In the process of seeing afresh the story of Abraham and the calf, Kushner—while pointing to the patriarch's discovery, in the Cave of Machpelah, of humanity's primal mother and father, the "embryonic garden," and the "path back to the One of Being"—brilliantly elaborates on the mysteries of parent-child relationships, sexuality and knowledge and death, the two voices of the Holy One (the voice without and the voice within), the revelation of silence, the genetic transmission of memory, the similarities between Kabbalistic and recent cosmological theories about the first light-blazing moments of the universe, the experiencing of and returning to Nothingness, and the reemergence from the cave to the world. "If the searcher chooses to remain with eternity," Kushner concludes, "the searcher loses eternity! If the searcher chooses this finite world, the searcher is rewarded with eternity! This is expressed in a slightly different way by the saying that the pious are not in paradise, paradise is in the pious. We do not know if the question was ever put to Abraham. We are told only that he returned to lunch."

* * *

The author of this extraordinary meditation on death and rebirth, Lawrence Kushner, was born in Detroit in 1943, studied philosophy at the University of Cincinnati, and was ordained as a reform rabbi from Hebrew Union College in 1969. Following his ordination, he served as a rabbinic fellow-in-residence at Congregation Solel in Highland Park, Illinois, and has been the rabbi at Congregation Beth El, Sudbury, Massachusetts, since 1971. Among his writings are four books: *The Book of Letters: A Mystical Alef-Bait* (Harper & Row, 1975), *Honey from the Rock: Ten Gates of Jewish Mysticism* (Harper & Row, 1977), *The River of Light* (Behrman House Publishers, 1981; Harper & Row, 1981), and *The*

Book of Miracles: A Young Person's Guide to Jewish Spirituality (Union of American Hebrew Congregations, 1987)—inspiring and profound works that have been praised by people such as I. B. Singer, Elie Wiesel, Rabbi Zalman Schachter, Malcolm Boyd, Baba Ram Das, and Robert Ornstein.

Lawrence Kushner lives with his wife and three children in Sudbury, Massachusetts—a suburb of Boston that adjoins the town of Natick.* Lawrence Kushner suggested that we do our interview over lunch in Boston on October 21, 1986—three days after the beginning of Sukkot. And before we started to eat (and talk), Rabbi Kushner said a blessing over the meal.

* * *

I know that in your school days you studied art and philosophy. What led you eventually to take the religious path?

My grandfather was a *classical* German reform Jew—three generations probably make me a blue blood! And my parents were pious reform Jews—which almost sounds like a contradiction in terms—but which is only to say that they went to Temple on Friday nights because that's what reform Jews were supposed to do. I do not think that I ever had a religious experience—no "Hallelujah Chorus," no lights flashing on and off. What I *did* have, though—and still have—was an insatiable curiosity about what was ultimately true and meaningful in life. Somehow, somewhere, *somebody* must have known something about it, though it seemed to be hidden.

It's like the story of the King who wanted his people to be close to him. He knew if he made it too easy, they'd give up the search. So he built for himself a magnificent but illusory castle, and then invited the people to come close to him. Because it was a challenge, they tried to approach, but because it was difficult, they gave up. Finally, however, the child of the King said, "These walls are an illusion!" And he proceeded to walk right through them until he found his father, the King.

Why did you decide to become a rabbi?

* The town of Natick's rabbi happens to be Harold Kushner, the best-selling author of *When Bad Things Happen to Good People.* The two rabbis know each other and study together on Monday mornings; but they are not related, and their published books are different both in style and approach.

When I first considered the rabbinate seriously, I was in high school. It seemed then like—and still does—a beautiful way to earn a living: To get paid for being with people during the most meaningful times of their lives and trying to help people make sense of them. And then to try to connect people with others who have *also* just gone through great life passages.

Of course, in that sense you might have just simply decided to have become a therapist.

But a therapist talks about these things *afterwards.* He or she says, to paraphrase Professor Jacob Needleman, "Let's figure out why you are the way you are." A rabbi says, "What will you do about it?" I'm the boatman. You come to me and say, "I want to get married." And I say, "I believe I can get you across the river. No guarantees. But I do know many of the currents and what to say." So you get in the boat, and I take you across. Then the next day, I meet someone who tells me, "My father has died." The next day someone else will say, "This baby just came into the universe, I need to know how to give it a name." The next day a kid will inform me, "I'm thirteen years old [which means he's sexually mature], I'm ready to become an adult, a *mensch.*" To each one of them I say, "I am honored to try to take you across, come on."

I guess that's the main reason I became a rabbi, and the main reason I stay with it now.

How did you happen to write your first book, The Book of Letters?

It's a funny story. Do you know *The Jewish Catalog?* It was modeled after the *Whole Earth Catalog,* was first published by three Brandeis University students in 1973, and was an enormous success. At the back of the book the editors wanted a list of people you could go to to be your teacher. I was invited to be listed as one of those teachers. I was just four years out of rabbinical school and was terribly honored. At the bottom of the invitation I was asked what I could teach somebody. I thought of suggesting *theology,* but I noticed Maurice Friedman's name with that subject; I thought of *social ethics,* but Arnold Wolf's name was beside that; then I considered *Hasidic stories,* but that was taken by the Lubavitcher *rebbe!* Who was I to offer to teach anything on such a distinguished list? So I decided to say, as a joke, that I could teach the Hebrew alphabet—the *Alef-bait.* The editors printed it straight. Soon I started to get phone calls from people who wanted me to teach them the *Alef-bait.* This led me to research the stories about how the letters are made and about their "personalities." You can't know Hebrew and see the letter *Bait,* for instance, without thinking of the word *Barukh* ("Blessed"). You might say that the names for Hebrew letters are like the names of cities. I can say "Dallas" or "Chicago," and there's a mood unique to each. It's the same with the letters. Ultimately, I put it all together in *The Book of Letters: A Mystical Alef-bait.*

It's been said that a noted eighteenth-century Talmudic scholar, afraid of losing his faith, came to seek the advice of the Hasidic master, the Maggid of Mezeritch. The Maggid did not engage the man in philosophy, but instead asked him to recite with him, over and over again, the very first prayer every Jewish child learns by heart. And that was all. I mention this story because it seems that simply learning or relearning the Hebrew alphabet may also provide such healing power and solace.

Perhaps the most sacred thing a Jewish teacher can do is to teach someone the letter *Alef*—the first letter—which has *almost* a sound—for it begins everything. As I say in *The Book of Letters,* "Open your mouth and begin to make a sound. STOP! That is *Alef.*" So to teach a child, or even an adult, *Alef* is to teach him or her the mother of all articulate speech—the beginning of all noise. As Gershom Scholem observes, it's the sound of the larynx clicking into gear . . . raw, undifferentiated noise, like the sound of the Shofar (which is just more audible). Everything is in it. Sometimes I suspect that everything I've ever written is in fact just a commentary on the letter *Alef*—an attempt to understand why the words for "fire" and "God" and "Adam" and "One" all begin with *Alef.*

It's important to realize that we are really the people of the Book— we come into being with the Word. In our psychospiritual tradition, God makes the world with words: "And God *said.*" Susan Handelman, in her important study *The Slayers of Moses,* comments that in Hellenistic and classical Christian thought, words are signs for perfect things up in heaven. But for the Jew, the word *is* ultimate reality, the most real thing there is. (The Hebrew word for "word"—*davar*—means "thing.") And as I mention in my *Book of Letters,* the letters of the alphabet exist independently of ink and paper or even words. We learn that when Moses shattered the first set of tablets, the letters ascended to the One who gave them. And in another place, the story is told of Rabbi Hananya ben Teradyon that he was wrapped in a scroll of the Torah and burned at the stake. Moments before his death, his students cried out, "Master!

What do you see?'' He answered, "The parchment is burning, but the letters are flying toward the heavens!"

Religious Jews, of course, believe that the Torah literally *contains the words of God.*

To say that Torah is an ultimate reality doesn't mean we should read it literally. (God wrote the Torah with his finger; can we ask, "Which finger?") If you push biblical stories to their literal extreme, they disintegrate. If you try to mix two stories so that there are no longer any contradictions between them, they both collapse. It is as if every story comes to teach only one thing! Or as if *all* the characters of a story aren't meant to be identified with! There are half a dozen different accounts of what happened at Sinai, and they all contradict each other. Which could mean that the person who put together the final version was a sloppy editor . . . or, what is much more likely, that he was aware of the multifaceted nature of holy moments.

What do you think of numerological approaches to the Torah and to sacred and mystical texts generally?

I remember a woman who came up to me after a lecture I'd given in Southern California and said, "Rabbi Kushner, I traveled to this lecture on the number forty-nine bus. What does that mean?" "Maybe it means something," I replied, "but I don't have any idea." Of course there are layers of meaning within everything, but most of them are inaccessible to us. Rabbi Zalman Schachter-Shalomi used to tell the story about a man who was born on May 5, 1905, was fifty-five years old, had five kids, lived on 555 Fifth Street, had $555,000 in the bank. One day he opened the newspaper and saw that a horse named Number Five was running in the fifth race that afternoon. So he called his bookie and said, "Put all my money on that horse." And you know what happened? He won. The horse came in fifth!

So, sure, there are all kinds of things going on in the universe, but if you try to "play" them, you are courting danger and madness. Actually, I suspect that this kind of magical mysticism is not really an attempt to understand the ultimate nature of reality but rather a way to manipulate it. It is pseudoscience and idolatrous. In the final analysis, for all our mysticism, there's you and I having lunch together. Are you a *mensch?* Am I a *mensch?* For *that* may be the really hard thing to be and the only thing that matters.

In a book entitled Aspects of the Hebrew Genius, *published in 1910, there is a chapter on Jewish mysticism by H. Sperling, in which the author writes: "They [the vague mystical yearnings of man] can, however, fitly be compared to that invisible chain that binds husband to wife, parents to children, relation to relation, friend to friend, social unit to social unit. Without these lesser mysticisms society would dissolve into its first atoms; without the larger mysticism man would break away from his Maker and be flung into nothingness." I imagine that you would agree.*

It *is* a wonderful quote. I'm reminded that just the other day, one of the eleventh-grade kids I teach asked me to explain God. I said: "If someone walked into your home and saw you and your family, he'd see that you and other members of your family were discrete and basically independent human beings. But if this visitor were very smart and very patient, he'd begin to discover that despite your independence you were also determined by invisible lines of relationship joining you to one another. And if he had a computer big enough to keep track of everything all of the time, he'd begin to realize that your behavior was much more organic in the context of a total family unit than it was as an individual.

"Now, all of this is fairly obvious, and something family-systems therapists take for granted. Ultimately, you'll connect increasingly larger circles of people. And, if you could just focus on this process long enough, you'd begin to discover that it would include *all* living things and eventually all Being. . . . So that's what we're talking about when we talk about God—an infinite series of glistening invisible threads that join every being with everything else in being . . . and that every once in a while, we catch a glimpse of this."

Now after I'd been trying to explain this, one of the kids in the class said excitedly, "I get it . . . *my* family and *your* family . . ." And another kid interrupted him and shouted out, "We have lift-off!" . . . Because all of a sudden he'd seen it too.

"From the highest rungs," you write in your second book, Honey from the Rock, *"everything is seen." And you add: "You can know nothing save what is intended. There is only avoiding or awareness."*

I think that maybe the closest Jews come to the notion of karma is: "It's meant to be"—for instance, that you and I are here today in Boston having lunch; and I know that I'll be changed by this meeting. Sometimes we just keep a reverent silence.

When you fall in love and for the first time you confess your love for one another, there's a moment in that mutual confession when you want to say, "Since before the creation of the world, it was meant to be that we should meet and carve our initials on the willow tree." You feel as if you're in the hands of forces that are much larger than you. And at *precisely* that moment—and here's the wonderful paradox—you feel freer than you've ever felt. I believe it was Martin Buber who used the phrase: You've "stepped into your destiny," you're now doing what is meant for you to do, and you're doing it with all of yourself—you're not holding anything back.

I was thinking that the notion of either "avoiding" or "becoming aware" certainly hits home when Oedipus, who runs away from his adopted home in order to avoid killing his father, later confesses: "And as I fled I reached that very spot/where the great king . . . met his death." And later Oedipus will say: "O god—/all come true, all burst to light!/O light—now let me look my last on you!/I stand revealed at last. . . ."

I was born with alternating isotropia—I only see with one eye at a time. (I tend to use one for far away and one for close up.) So for me, vision is a very complicated process. It has always fascinated me that mystics have a *vision* while prophets *hear* the voice of God. Notice how easily we move from the letter *Alef*—the beginnings of all sound—to light—the needle-thin beam of light that can both pierce the darkness and blind a person.

When people ask Oedipus not to inquire further into the mystery of his identity, he says: "What? . . . Fail to solve the mystery of my birth? Not for all the world!" Similarly, Abraham—as you describe him in The River of Light, *seeks out the origins of his—and humanity's—psyche by entering the Cave of Machpelah, where he encounters our primal parents, Adam and Eve.*

To know what Adam and Eve knew . . . it's the forbidden wisdom. It is the secret of life, and if you discover it, you die. God says, "If you eat from this tree, you'll discover the secret of life." I believe that sexuality itself is only a metaphor for something we don't yet understand, something deeper, something about the nature of being. We haven't yet found the urtext for sexuality—the creation of life . . . procreation.

But it also seems connected to the fact of death.

Childhood is a garden of Eden. The beginning of the end is when you become a sexual being. Your parents say, "If you learn how to 'do it,' we're going to kick you out of the house, childhood will end, and you're going to die." You're not a dummy, so you reply, "It's pretty nice staying at home. I think I won't learn about how to do it. I'll just hang around and be a good little boy." But sooner or later just about everyone says, "I would rather die than not know how to 'do it'." So you're on your own and mortal with the paradoxical comfort that sexuality enables you to be immortal.

The psychologist Michael Gruber has pointed to the connection between the words "genesis" and "genitalia."

In Hebrew, the first word of *Genesis* is *B'raysheet.* It begins with the Hebrew letter *Bait,* which means "in, with, or by." *B'raysheet* is usually translated, "In the beginning." But you could also translate it as: "With *raysheet* God created the heavens and the earth." One tradition suggests that *raysheet* is another name for Torah—a preexistent wisdom, an ultimate light. And that's what God used to make the world with—ultimate light. The Aramaic idiom for a blind man, literally, means "one full of light." The same image.

Like the all-knowing Tiresias, to whom Oedipus benightedly says: "Blind,/lost in the night, endless night that nursed you!/You can't hurt me or anyone else who sees the light—".

Exactly.

Light for you is obviously a metaphor for spiritual awareness—the light by which we see the light. And in The River of Light *you write: "To become aware is to join the Holy One in the act of creating oneself."*

There is an old Hasidic story about a man who's been dead for four years but doesn't know it! When you become aware, you become alive again. But you can't endure being aware for more than a moment . . .

208

it would be like breathing pure oxygen, or like being blinded by the light.

Cosmologists have speculated that at the first explosive moment of the birth of the universe, everything that exists—or ever will exist—was contained within a single spark of energy, smaller than an atom's nucleus and ruled by a single primordial law.

One dot—a point of light. Perhaps the fact that the contemporary cosmologists talk about a dimensionless point of light from which all being sprang and that the Kabbalists long ago came up with precisely the same image (in the fourteenth century, Moses de Leon spoke of "a hidden, supernal point" whose "primal center is the innermost light, of a translucence, subtlety, and purity beyond comprehension") means that this awareness comes from something we all carry within us. We're walking Torahs, it's in our DNA . . . if we could just shut up and listen to it. As Rabbi Dov Baer of Mezritch said: "I shall teach you the best way to say Torah. You must cease to be aware of yourselves. You must be nothing but an ear which hears what the universe of the word is constantly saying within you."

In **The River of Light** *you state: "The dream awakens even though the one who dreams remains asleep." As if to say that on some level we are aware even when we aren't.*

There are two kinds of dreams. One is the phantasmagoric dream. The other is the Great Dream. It is a dimension of God—it's one of the ways we encounter the Holy One. The Great Dream and the River of Light are the same.

You yourself often suggest that Scripture itself is a Great Dream.

In *The River of Light* I try to show some of the connections between and among Torah and Dream and God. You see, we're warned not to make the Torah a sanctified object. But people *do* kiss it when they carry it. They dress and undress it. One could make a case for Torah being a feminine expression of God. In the words of the *Zohar* [a Kabbalistic commentary on the Bible written by Moses de Leon in late-thirteenth-century Spain]: "For the Torah resembles a beautiful and stately damsel, who is hidden in a secluded chamber of her palace and who has a secret lover, unknown to all others. For love of her he keeps passing the gate of her house, looking this way and that in search of her. She knows that her lover haunts the gate of her house. What does she do? She opens the door of her hidden chamber ever so little, and for a moment reveals her face to her lover, but hides it again forthwith."

In The River of Light *you interpret Scripture the way therapists interpret dreams.*

I think that the more analyzable something is, the more it partakes of holiness.

"A dream uninterpreted is like a letter undeciphered," says the Zohar.

Imagine having a handwritten letter from an interesting person whom you've never met just lying on your mantel, and you don't open it. You want to read it, but you don't. What would that mean?

It would be as if Abraham, when he saw the calf run into the Cave, got nervous about following it. . . .

And then decided to get another calf. Exactly. . . . The reason Abe discovers what he does is because of his ability to pay attention, to open elaborately sealed letters.

When God wanted to get Moses' attention, He decided to make a bush burn and not be consumed. Now, everyone says the burning bush was a miracle. But that wasn't as big a miracle as having the Red Sea split or the sun stand still. Compared to them, it was a cheap trick. One day, while wondering about why God would use such a trick, I began to watch a fire burning in the fireplace. Do you know how long you have to observe dry kindling wood burn in order to know whether or not it's going to be consumed? Five to seven minutes. That's how long it would have taken Moses to realize that the burning bush wasn't going to be consumed. But when was the last time you *really* looked at something for that long?

So I figure the burning bush wasn't a miracle at all, it was a *test*. God wanted to see if God was dealing with someone who could pay attention for more than five minutes. Once God realized that Moses could do that, God talked to him. And my theory is that if I *myself* could pay attention to anything for five minutes, God would talk to me, too! But so far, I haven't been able to do it.

In **Honey from the Rock** *you talk about "losing the narrative element of our existence." And in* **The River of Light** *you describe Abraham leaving the narrative of his life, as he enters the Cave, only to return to it after he has had his vision.*

That's the Jewish model: You come back to the rest of the characters in the story and have lunch. All stories are metaphors for God. When you enter them, you're doing a very religious thing. And the Great Dream, like God, is the place in which you discover where everything is connected, all the stories fit together. In the image of the Kabbalists, all the words of the Torah will be pronounceable as one long name of God.

When I think of your statement that "The dream awakens even though the one who dreams remains asleep," I can't help but be reminded of the story of one such dreamer—Jacob at Bethel—who used a stone as his pillow and dreamt one night of a ladder—its foot on the earth, its top touching the heavens—with angels going up and down the rungs. And when he woke up the next morning, Jacob cried out: "God is surely here, and I did not know."

I'm presently working on a book that's a kind of theological novel. And its thesis is that, in the same way that when every bride and groom stand under the *chupah* [wedding canopy] they are joined by Eve and Adam and all the other brides and grooms who ever stood under the *chupah;* or, in the same way, that when you visit a battlefield and stand there quietly for a moment, all the soldiers who fought and died there are there with you; so when you have a great insight into the nature of being, all the people who also had that same insight throughout history come and join you. (Oedipus, for example, was at lunch with us today.)

The focus of the book will be Jacob at Bethel. As you said, he goes to sleep in what he thinks is a godforsaken place, has the dream of the angels ascending and descending a ladder, wakes up, and says, "God is surely here, and I did not know." There are many different ways that statement can be understood, all of which are true to the original Hebrew and touch on some of the possibilities of what it could mean to talk about God and to be spiritually aware.

This is how we write what Jacob said in Hebrew [writes it out], and here's how I'd transliterate it: *Awchayn yesh Adonai ba-makom ha-zeh v-anochi lo yadati. Awchayn* is usually translated as "surely," but I translate it as "Wow!" *Yesh* is "really," *Adonai* is "God," *ba-makom ha-zeh* is "in this place" or "here." Then: *v-* ("and") *anochi* ("I"), and *lo* ("not") *yadati* ("I knew"). . . . So we have: "Wow! God is really here, and I . . . I knew not."

Now, the simplest level of interpreting this is that given by Rashi [the eleventh-century commentator of the Bible and the Talmud], who says that what Jacob's statement means is: "If I had known God had been here, I wouldn't have gone to sleep"—a simple but profound interpretation. Or, as the kids in my youth group say, "Most of the time the lights are on but nobody's home."

On another level, you can read these words to mean: "Wow, God was here because my I, I did not know" . . . which is to say: "The reason God was here was because I was not aware I was me—the self-reflexive part of myself shut down." So a tremendous awareness occurs but without the sense of one's self having appropriated it.

On the third level, the *Zohar* says: "God was here with the name *Anochi.*" Jacob didn't know until that moment that the universe had a Self and that its name was the name of the first-person singular pronoun —*Anochi*—which was the first word God said at Mt. Sinai ("I AM"). So, according to the *Zohar,* Jacob met the name of the Self of the universe and realized that there is an "I" to being that has an order and a plan.

Then on the fourth level, we can talk about the despair found in the words "God was here, and I didn't know it." In the depths of despair there is a light that shines; and that as terrible as you might feel, what one discovers is that God is in that despair, too, and that you carry within you the seeds of your own redemption. You can take a deep breath and trust yourself because God is there.

Now, there are several other levels. But the one I finally want to mention is that given by a rabbi named Shimshon ben Pesach Ostropoler—a mystic who was killed in a pogrom in 1648 in the Ukraine—who said that what Jacob *really* saw in his dream that night was the *Merkavah*—the Celestial Chariot originally seen and described by Ezekiel. Jacob had always thought that the Chariot was carried by three creatures—a lion, a cherub, and an eagle. Now, the first letter of "lion" in Hebrew is *Alef,* the first letter of "cherub" is *Kaf,* and the first letter of "eagle" is *Nun*—which spells *Awchayn.* So we can read Jacob's statement as: "Lion, cherub, and eagle were in this place." These same letters, moreover, are also in *v-anochi*—along with the fourth letter, a *Yud.* So Jacob realizes, "Wow! The *Yud* is the first letter of *my* name." And suddenly he becomes aware that it was *he* who was the fourth person carrying the Chariot, and that *his* hands were God's hands. . . . Which completely blows Jacob away.

And me too! It's amazing what mysteries lie in these letters and words.

Just this past Shabbos morning I was teaching a class on *Ecclesiastes*—which is traditionally assigned to be read during this Sukkot season—and my students and I figured out a better translation of the opening refrain: "Vanity of vanities; all is vanity." What we came up with was: "Breath on the mirror, breath on the mirror, all life is breath on the mirror."

It *is* fleeting, it's just *fleeting* . . . and what doesn't seem clear now will be clear later. Because ultimately all we have is awareness. That's our only hope. Eyes wide open. Made for wonder.

[Boston, 1986]